This book is dedicated to the brethrens of

Via Vera Cruz Nocturna

With a special appreciation to the priceless support of
Bo Mambo Mama Tida Chouquet, Nigel A. Jackson, Shani Oates & Jesse
Louis Hathaway. Also; great gratitude is due to Mogg Morgan for his
keen editorial eye and the enthusiasm that made this work manifest.May
you all be Kings and Queens, Now and Forever more!

FRONTISPIECE: LUCIFER - AUDREY MELO

The Craft of the Untamed

Nicholaj de Mattos Frisvold

Mandrake of Oxford

Published by
Mandrake of Oxford
PO Box 250
OXFORD
OX1 1AP (UK)

Contents

Foreword by Shani Oates 7

Introduction 11

1   At the Crossroads of the Worlds 15

2   Solomonic Magick 23

3   The Blood of the Living Bones 47

4   Within the Mountain of Dame Venus 74

5   The Vinculum of Eros 98

6   The Art of Timeless Tradition 119

7   Within the Veil of Night 143

8   Against the Current 161

Farewell 169

Selected Bibliography 172

Notes 177

Index 179

SETE ESPIRITOS - AUDREY MELO

Foreword

Occultists and mystics have for many centuries debated recurring yet transient qualities of what constitutes the core issues of belief and practice, especially within the Craft. Orthodox theology becomes grafted onto heterodox psychology – an alchemical fusion that sparks a bold genre of enquiry. So, naturally seeking commensurate responses, we are obliged to ask, where exactly then, do we encounter the Nocturnal Mysterium? In our Hearts? Possibly. Within the Mind? Probably. Or, more presumably, within the 'Other?' Once there, how do we relate to the numinous and at what point does instinct become concatenate with intuition. Comprehension of such anomalies occurs only through direct apprehension via the Source.

Groping blindly we hope to reach the Tree of Gnosis, thereto stand beneath its fragrant boughs, to catch the leaves that formulate 'The Book of Wisdom,' the hoary tome that quickens the blood, when word of it is whispered across the halls and corridors of temples, nemetons and holy places. Words here stir a maelstrom within each reader anew. Ideas drawn from compound truths cast wide the influence of their magic. Profound messages compel great deeds of variant fortune, subject as they are to the winds of Fate in all Her guises.

Too few books have emerged that regard or even consider a valid expression of Craft Traditions, even fewer by academics who actually practise meaningfully the fruits of their studies. Fewer still engage in the Gnosis generated by that fusion of Mind and Spirit with the enigmatic World Soul, the Anima Mundi, wherein the Magus becomes a locus for his supreme arte. The genesis of expression formulates a template for pleromic realisation activated within the intuitive reader. This book is primed through the innovative lens of radical psychologist, Dr. Nicholaj de Mattos Frisvold, who boldly utilises his expertise to explore fundamental keys that offer compelling vistas through which the reader may participate in this nebulous and enigmatic 'Otherworld' of shadows.

Force breathes through all form. Green leaves are enlivened by mystical subtlety as ink records a grand narrative style, albeit in the Traditional sense. A grammar of erudition, of insight and informed practise – Dr Frisvold describes a portal through which the voyeur may peer into a subjective perspective, over the threshold of subliminal normality, inviting them, like Alice, through the looking glass. A visionary landscape presents a reversal of all that is known for all that is not, all that is true for all that is not – a 'wyrd' journey in the absolute sense.

Language engages the reader, drawn in by the writer's craft to partake on a conscious level some understanding of the afore-mentioned 'Otherworld.' Using poetic nuances in tandem with his adeptness within his given field of professional psychology, Dr Frisvold leads us through a descent journey, where seven levels are traversed to enact the primal exchange between God and man. Moments of repose and action generate the *'scala philosophorum'* and the seven circuit labyrinth, whose pathways and platforms weave us forward into the arc of all potentiality.

Force yields transparency to the Compass, where practical advice persuades ritual activity to counter the often baffling and intrepid triangulations of dry form elsewhere found. Cain and Seth, bearers of the Twin Pillars receive un-prejudicial expression through the Mysteries also associated with Apollo and Dionysus who merge into a harmonic unity embraced upon the Via Vera Cruz. We hunger for return; we the progeny of the so called 'fallen' yearn for respite, for reunion, for re-entry into the emblazoned cusp of all luminal reality. Thus do we push towards the juncture of fire and ice, into the faerie mounds, to rend the Veil of the nebulous 'Other.' Barriers to realisation restore the stigma of exile.

Yet Gnosis is not acquired through learning, but from understanding. Understanding is imparted through experience alone! And experience occurs only through literal engagement within sacred space, essentially the crux, the point upon the crossroads, or Qutub of potentialities. Moreover, within this implicit genesis, a centrifugal force pulses into play leading out all leapers-in-between , dancing towards the edge of the abyss, where the void transmutes all kinetic energy into streams of light – kalas upon the miasmic web, the Matrix of Being within the Void of Non-Being.

The Work becomes a celebration of the liberations from the bounds of ignorance, expressing the Virtue of Truth that in its unveiling, filters illumination, the guide to enlightenment. Exploration of these truths brings an awareness that hones our perception of the roles and reality of the Trickster, the Sage, the Master and the Servant, the Devil and the Lord into sharp focus as the guard and guide of all who seek True Unity, and not the mundane and erroneous polarity, or worse – a duality. Such artificial limitations negate fruition of The Work.

Imperative landscapes are skilfully navigated and chartered. Most particularly, the Wilderness of ingress and the congress of the Wasteland as elements germane to the Mysteries are alluded to, suggested, or expressed in collusion with relevant themes. The Muse is also the Harpy; Her two faces reflect the Pale and the Dark aspects of the female numen exemplified best in the Spinner and the Reaper. Candidly, Dr Frisvold dispatches erroneous misconceptions that diverge from the central point of Truth. Craft ancestries of blood and bone, kith and kin, hearth and home become revealed in their glorious primality. Critically, this tenacious and uncompromising study, supported by manifold expertise is given expression through the synergistic field mediums of occultism, folklore and astrology.

Within the Appendices, themes of surrender and will stimulate the dynamic between Horizon and Abyss, Ordeal and Ardour and the hierarchy of the Golden Chain of being. All these potencies develop into a purposeful backdrop for the journey of the Pilgrim as they are guided upon the path of One by the Higher Self or (Agatho) Daimon who challenges the aspirant in their understanding of true ingress as that which is beyond, and not within the Self. Bravely Dr. Frisvold pursues causalities and praxes misappropriated throughout the Craft, facilitating the eventual purpose and realisation of the Via Vera Cruz.

Shani Oates, Maid of The Clan of Tubal Cain, Martinmas, 2010

Introduction

This book about Traditional Craft is informed by a wide range of studies, both from individuals and textual research. I had the pleasure of rewarding friendships and apprenticeships with practitioners of the nameless Art in the Isle of Albion, Scandinavia, Italy, Haiti, Nigeria and Brazil. The presentation of Traditional Craft you are about to venture into is not solely as presented by British and Scandinavian practitioners, it is also coloured extensively by traditional and hereditary Craft lineages from Italy and Brazil. I have found the themes related to the crossroad, to the dead, to the powers of the night as well as the origin and goal of the Craft strikingly similar in their diverse expressions. It is these common motives I will present in this book.

Many contemporary presentations of this subject take an eclectic approach, which often leads to an uncritical use of myths and legends. This distinctively modern approach is often accompanied by an erroneous use of etymology and epistemology where phenomena are taken out of context and given distorted meaning. In light of this, it is important to point out that I consider myself a traditionalist and consequently I focus on unity and non-dualism – as passed down through the legacy and "race" of Seth.[1]

This demands some clarification. Seth was the third son of Adam and Eve, the replacement of Abel. In this Seth can be seen as the unification of the opposing poles represented by Abel and Cain. This perspective naturally leads to an interest for the Craft as practiced by peasants and dwellers in the countryside. As such the word 'tradition' is exemplified in the works of Plato and the *Hermetica*. Traditional Craft is always signified by some sort of otherworldly contact, guidance and apprenticeship, whether this be in the Hollow Hills, Venus Mountain, the Sabbath, 'the Kingdom' or Elphame where the Sidhe or Faery teach. It is from this communion with the faeries or nymphs that the Craft originates. What we refer to as traditional Craft is actually the art of otherworldly interaction, where visible and invisible nature interact as partakers of the same world.

This position I have taken will probably benefit from some more clarification as it will affect one integral part of modern traditional witchcraft, the modern Luciferian phenomena. Lucifer-Lumiel is subject for a certain richness of myths that claim some sort of precedence. Lucifer is alternatively an angel that oversees the process of the fall and the patron of the maleficas of night and misanthropy. In the infantile ramblings of St. Jerome, Lucifer is equated with Satan. This gives Lucifer properties ranging from a vile misanthropic angel and the source for enlightenment for humankind. The Biblical passage Isaiah 14:12 that speaks of Lucifer, equates him with Venus, the Morningstar and the fallen angels:

"How art thou fallen from heaven, O Lucifer, son of the Morning".

The Prophet Isaiah, who experienced the captivity of the Hebrews in Babylon and fought for their freedom delivered this message to king Nebuchadnezzar. Isaiah saw the king's pride as hubris. Hubris is a specific form of pride, the root of all sin, a misplaced sense of self-importance. Hubris in antiquity was considered to be worthy of death provoking the Goddess Nemesis to execute judgement.

The idea of fallen angels entered Christian theology after Dionysus penned his exposition on 'The Celestial hierarchies' in the 5th Century. Here a predominantly Gnostic idea of ascent became subject to a fall. Hubris, improper pride, was transposed as the primal and most cardinal of all sins and thus a link was forged with Lucifer-Satan as the angel whose fall was caused by hubris.

Prior to these medieval ideas spirits followed hierarchies and there were no great focus on the angelic fall. You might protest that the *Book of Enoch* presents the idea of a fall. These angels were "The Watchers of Heaven" or *grigori*, their function was to watch, observe, guide and instruct mankind. This function can at times be experienced as a transgression as they take humans as students in the "Angelic Arts".

The fall seems to be much more related to the desire for something that is not in harmony with one's constitution or destiny. I might suggest that it was a desire for corporality and the pleasures of Eros that was their fall. Not because sexuality is particularly evil, but because it deflected the angels from their station and destiny. It follows from this that a fall, from a traditional perspective, is to abandon one's destiny and station. This leads to questions concerning restoration and how a fall in the celestial hierarchies affects the world of men.

Isaiah's, celestial world mirrored the world of men. It is important to reflect upon this as it is crucial to understand the fundamentals of the Craft. Isaiah's lament was aimed at the king of Babylon. All royalty in antiquity and up to the Renaissance was seen as manifestations of divine principles or deities. The Pharaoh Thutmose was seen as a reincarnation of Thoth; Julius Caesar as the son of Venus; Elizabeth I as a manifestation of the Virgin-Mother and Alexander the Great was seen as Zeus and Ammon, and as Ammon he was in Muslim lore identified with Shaitan.

Culture conditions us to look at the world and the past in a particular way. While the traditional worldview sees the connectedness of all things;

the modern worldview looks inwards and finds individuality. The spiritual quest aims to manifest the indwelling God, often neglecting the spiritual hierarchy. We might say that modern man is forfeiting his destiny in favour of his ambition and lust, and in this the essential nature of the fall plays itself out again and again.

There is no unity, merely an ambitious drive towards what is hidden within each individual, in order to become a fully realized human being. This realization relies what is suppressed inside of us.

My intention in this book is to present the main pillars of Traditional Witchcraft on the premise of unity. I will present the nature of the Craft free for needless obscuration. By doing this it is my hope that the Wise Arts and the powers of the denizens of the night will be accessible and valued for their own rare beauty and power.

1

At the Crossroads
of the Worlds

"The Horned Master governs the generative powers of the kingdom of the beasts, the raw forces of life, death and renewal which sustains the natural world." -Nigel A Jackson. The Call of the Horned Piper: 38

The Art and Craft of the Witches is found at the crossroad, where this world and the other side meets and all possibility become reality. This simple fact is often forgotten as one rushes to the Sabbath or occupies oneself with formalities of ritual. The cross marks the four quarters, the four elements, the path of Sun, Moon and Stars. The cross was fused or confused with the Greek *staurus*, meaning 'rod', 'rood' or 'pole'. Various forms of phallic worship are simply, veneration for the cosmic point of possibility and becoming. It is at the crossroads we will gain all or lose all and it is natural that it is at the crossroads we gain perspective.

The crossroad is a place of choice, the spirit-denizens of the crossroads are said to be tricky and unreliable and it is of course where we find the Devil.

One of the most famous legends of recent times concerns the blues-man Robert Johnson (1911–1938). He claimed that, one night, just before midnight he had gone to the crossroads. He took out his guitar and played, whereupon a big black guy appeared, tuned his guitar, played a song backwards and handed it back.[2] This incident altered Johnson's playing and his finest and most everlasting compositions were the fruit of the few years of life left to him. This legend tells us how he needed to bury himself at the crossroads, offering himself to the powers dwelling there.

Business done with the Devil is said to give him the upper hand. The ill omens and *malefica* associated with such deals is present in Johnson's story. He got fame and women, but he died less than three years later before he reached thirty. His body was found poisoned at a crossroads, the murderer's identity a mystery. Around the Mississippi no less than three tombs carry the name of Robert Leroy Johnson.

The image of the Devil remains one of threat, blessing, beauty and opportunity. Where we find the Devil we find danger, unpredictability and chaos. If he offers a deal we know we are in for a complicated bargain.

The Devil says that change is good, that we need movement in order to progress. His world is about cunning and ordeal entwined like the serpents of past and future on the pole of ascent.

It is to the crossroads we go to make decisions. It is at the crossroads we set the course for the journey. It is at the crossroads we confront ourselves and realize our power. At the crossroads we can descend to the land of death or ascend to the celestial fields.

The crossroad is the realm of communion. Resistance to change has given the Devil a bad reputation. His enigmatic ways of securing growth and movement has created an array of negative, morally challenged terms. But morality is no field for the Devil. Choices that instead of blessings bring lessons are of the Devil's making.

The Yoruba in West Africa believe that *Esu Yangi* lives at the crossroad. *Esu* is the power of transformation and movement, and this particular

Esu is associated with the red and worn dust found at the crossroad. This dust carries the power of good decisions and provokes the better choice. People go to the crossroad or take this dust and through ritual acts and words of power elevate its properties and spirit. They ignite the fire of transformation. The Yoruba see bad decisions as not being aligned with destiny.

The Devil has the power to help with this alignment. His ways are of the night, of enigma and of challenge. He facilitates any form of growth and movement. He is the double edged sword, the blade that cuts both ways. The downward facing dagger is the cross beneath our feet the dual nature of the Devil.

The Horned Master with his reddened hue, horns and stang meet us at the crossroad. The moment we reject the Devil as a sinister and vile figure, an enemy of man, we are revealing our own ignorance. This reflects the ecclesiastical demonization of the spirits of night. To see the Devil as "Satan" is to renounce terrestrial nature with all its change and renewal.

What is in a Forked Road?

The world tree and the pole can both be understood to be a crossroad. The intersection of two or more lines, a track that suddenly reveals another, the Fairy-feet in the pastures marking the ley lines, the axis of the world tree, the very symbol of sacrifice and wisdom. The world tree and the pole can both be understood to be a crossroad. Man sees himself at a crossroad of his life in times of great change and confusion. At the crossroad the restless dead rise and powers from above and below commune.

People tried for witchcraft, and sorcery were once thought to be in allegiance with devils. These devils were Satan, Ashtaroth or some other demonic entity. Or fairies, the un-dead or the spirit of dead people. The Devil was attended by a host of demonic servants that he could send forth to do his work and bidding. While the kingdom of God was signified by unity and order, that of the Devil was its reversal, a realm of immorality, diversity and chaos.

The Devil did not restrict his work and mission to the dwellers of the countryside. The works of the Devil started in the Church and initially took the form of heresy. The period known as 'the witch craze' took hold during the intense changes the Church went through in the Middle Ages, and the Reformation. The witch hunts occurred just as much inside the Church as outside. For instance, in the trials of the Jesuit Father John-Baptist Girard in the mid 1600s we find the exorcism of Miss Mary-Catherine Cadiere, where Girard was accused of incest, abortion and sorcery. The priest had exorcised devils, but also invited more in – particularly of lust and obsession.[3]

Likewise, in the same period, Joan Peterson, known as the Witch of Wapping, was hanged in 1652 for the practice of malign witchcraft. The prosecution was preoccupied with outlandish visitors and shape-shifter. Several people reported that they had seen the Devil taking various forms such as dog and squirrel, and Peterson taking the form of a cat to harm children. The prosecution were interested in the accounts of the Devil coming to 'suck her'. We see here the motif of the familiar in the guise of a vampire. Her danger to the children arose from her powers of bewitchment or 'fascinatio'.

The power of 'fascinatio', has been ascribed to saints, sages, saddhus, sheiks and other wise people. Rabbis were reputed to be able with a glance from their eyes to dissolve people by fire. The source of the power was more important than the nature of the power itself. In the case of 'fascinatio' or 'the evil eye' this power was understood to be provoked by envious demons. This idea coloured the view held by the Fathers of the Church, which equated the demonic and the 'pagan' with Judaism.[4]   Since the founding fathers of the Church a separation between the civilized and natural took form. An orderly society claimed authority on the basis of its institutionalized schooling and stability, while the unruly powers in the wilderness create fear.

Modern researchers, especially Norman Cohn, have focused on the fear and paranoia in the trials of European witches in the 15th to 17th Century. Irrational observations generate some sort of paranoid truth. One of the more fierce testimonies in the case of Joan Peterson was of a baker. The baker swore that upon seeing a particular black cat he was overwhelmed by unnatural fear. The fear was so irrational that it could only be explained by the witch - shapeshifting into a cat! Fear, both rational and irrational contribute to an understanding of the more absurd allegations.

If we turn to Vodou in Haiti, we find African faith and philosophy blended with French cunning Craft and Masonry. Vodou possesses a feeling for the natural hierarchies and a cosmology that is a purer tradition than found in many of its sister religions. This is due in part to its reaction to oppression and revolution.

The idea of the crossroad as an inter-dimensional portal has been integrated into Vodou both from French sorcery and African cosmologies. The crossroad is understood from mutually enriching angles. These impulses have forged a deep and dynamic understanding of the crossroad as the intersection of all possibility.

At the Vodou crossroad we find Legba, also known as, Petwo Legba and his unruly counterpart, Kalfou. We also have Baron Samedi represented by the cross.

Legba has a variety of manifestations significant for the crossroad, he is Atibon, the form of Legba that most people meet early on in their Vodoun path – he is also Gran Chemin – "the Highway", denoting the importance of ascent and descent. Legba Kalfou is reminiscent of the murky image of the European Devil as he presides over the art of sorcery sending out legions of his three horned bull-shaped devils to execute his will.

The spirit signatures of the various Lwa, is structured around the basic form of the crossroad. At the crossroad we realize unity and move forward to where miracles are possible.

Legba is possibility and the Master of Chance as well as doorways and gateways. Through Legba we can walk within the fields of Gran Bwa, the Owner of Leaves and the Forest; and meet Baron Samedi, the Lord of Death and Sex, who typifies the enigma of life itself. At the crossroad we encounter the powers that follow us on our chosen path.

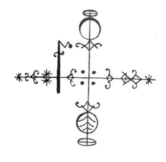

VEVE OF LEGBA

Radical consequences are encountered by entreating the crossroad and its powers. This is evident in the Cult of Exu, known as Kimbanda in Brazil. Here the Lord of the Crossroad has been given a classical diabolic image, a prankster and a foul-mouthed adversary that feeds on peppers, tobacco and hot drinks.

In times of need the people turn to Exu for advice, to gain the necessary power to cast spells. In the kingdom of Exu, the crossroad, people experience the irony of life's problems and find answers and solutions.

This is not far from the reality of the European witches. What the *kihuendes* (sorcerers) and *tatas* (priests) of the Cult of Exu refer to as 'the kingdom' shares profound similarities with the Witches' Sabbath. The crossroad is the point of entrance for sabbatical congress and the crossroad of Exu is the gate to his kingdom.

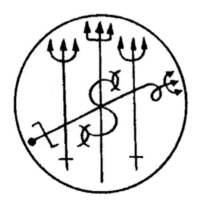

Ponto Riscado of Exu Meia Noite

REUNIÃO NO ANEL BY *AUDREY MELO*

2

Solomonic Magic

The demonic has for our western occult culture become linked extensively with the Lesser Key of King Solomon or Goetia. A similar text called *The Testament of Solomon* dates from around the 2nd Century and is the blueprint for this tradition. Basically the text tells of a vampyric and aggressive spirit that seeks to devour a young boy. King Solomon defends him, using a ring from the Archangel Michael. The book catalogues a number of spirits of an unruly and chaotic nature. The main spirit is Ornias and is described in the 44th verse:

> *"And he answered me: 'I, O King Solomon, am wholly voice, for I have inherited the voices of many men. For in the case of all men who are called dumb, it is I who smashed their heads, when they were children and had reached their eighth day. Then when a child is crying in the night, I become a spirit, and glide by means of his voice . . . In the crossways also I have many services to render, and my encounter is fraught with harm. For I grasp in all(?) instant a man's head, and with my hands, as with a sword, I cut it off, and put it on to myself. And in this way, by means of the fire which is in me, through my neck it is swallowed up.' "*

The Testament of Solomon is an interesting document, the foundation of the catalogue of spirits found in the Lemegeton, also called the Lesser Key of Solomon or Goetia. It might be that Ornias is the Marquis Orias in the Lemegeton, the 59th spirit, who as all other Marquis take his powers from the Moon.

Orias rides a horse and is said to hold two hissing serpents in his hands. His form is a hybrid of lion and serpent, the iconography of devils.

Contrary to the passage in the Testament of Solomon, the Lemegeton depicts Orias as a reconciler and teacher of the virtues of the stars, especially the mansions of the Moon. The Testament refers to the critical seven days prior to circumcision in rabbinical lore, presided over by Demon Queens such as Lilith, Mahaleth and Naamah. This suggests a common heritage from the folklore of the Hebrews.

Vampyric seizers also occur in The Testament of Solomon. Furthermore the sigil, of Orias bears a forked stave in its centre, perhaps a reference to the crossroad as a place where roads meet and part.

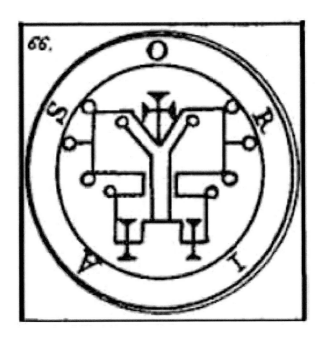

THE SEAL OF ORIAS

The Romans had several words for crossroad, for instance *bifrons* (two ways), *trifrons* (three ways) and *quadrofrons* (four ways). This is the realm of Janus, a legacy Hecate inherited with three roads meeting and parting.

Amongst the Yoruba, the threefold crossroad is particularly sacred to the Mothers of the Night, whilst the four ways is of particular importance to Esu. Trees are also important for the Mothers of the Night, as well as long beaked birds and raptors.

The crossroad is where pacts are made. In a *Book of St. Cyprian*[5] from Norway dating to 1780 we find the following formulae:

> *Go to the crossroad three Thursday nights in a row and say three times:*
>
> *Lucifer, Ac, Ac, Ac. The third night he will come silently to ask you what you want. He will answer that if you sign the contract in your own blood, he will do everything you wish and accomplish all that you demand. The contract is as follows.*

> *"I, N.N. demand your Service, you young Lucifer and the warden of Lukemborg, by the Living God. As long as you are obedient, I will be yours with life and blood – until eternity, body and soul and in death, I will be yours – in eternity, and I will not myself touch a hair on my head. No change or exorcism will you hear from me, as long as you accomplish all what I demand from you. And to these ends I sign with my own blood, that I renounce to serve the Creator and the Holy Trinity neither in word or sacraments, neither in life or living, night or day, asleep or awake, young or old, until my time of Death. Then it will all be yours, by the blood of the one who have signed."* [6]

There are a host of procedures for renouncing God, dating back to the same time. The renunciation of God is a prerequisite for the pact. You will need to rise up from sleep in the name of the Devil, to dress in the Devil and so forth. The whole day prior to the encounters at the crossroad will be a 'hallowing' in itself, a period of altering consciousness to receive and see the Devil. This dedication in words and actions will be noted by the Devil and he will see that you are firm in your intentions.

The following renunciation calls "the angels of the pit" on whatever morning you awake and follow the procedure in honour to the Devil. The renunciation procedure requires you continue to say the Lord's Prayer after each act of devilish praise. This would serve as an aid for transmitting great power, The "Father" of the prayer will be associated with the Devil:

> *"I renounce you my God that created me. I renounce you, Jesus, who redeemed me. I renounce God the Trinity that made me Holy. I will never more worship thee or serve you anymore after this very day, this I swear by my body and blood as the Young Lucifer, the greatest of the angels of the pit and chief, I swear my loyalty under his reign. He will therefore serve me in all what I demand to do and then I will sign this with my own blood as a safekeeping and security of my word, on the condition that he is carrying out all that I command and demand, then I will sign this contract with my own hand and in my own blood."* [7]

The Black Man in the Meadows of Possibility

The idea of Satan as the Arch-Devil continues to fascinate and intrigue. In 1999 the Vatican revised their liturgical procedure and added various psychological interpretations of possession and obsession. All forms of moral decay are ascribed to the Devil in his guise of Satan. The truth is that a personified Satan has always been the unofficial emissary of the Church, the Holy Scapegoat that scares many into the embrace of the Church. Thus with the aid of "Satan" people become loyal servants to a ruthless God obsessed with moral purity.

The identification of the Lord of Greenwood and Satan as the adversary of God was accomplished with the publication of 'Malleus Maleficarum' in 1486. According to the French historian Jules Michelet, the compendium, the handiwork of the imbecile monks Kramer and Sprenger, set the standard for demonological belief. It systemized the contents of Johannes Nider's *Formicarius* (1437) with some additional material mainly from German and Italian sources. This compendium on witch finding and *malefica* set down the theological foundation for Satan's power as a consequence of the fall of God's angels.

The differences between devils and demons became blurred in the same way as the division between the Devil and Satan. The message would be the same - everything pertaining to 'the other side' was vile, dangerous and would lead to no good. Those who convened with the powers of the other side were therefore up to no good and there was a theological reason to assume these people were witches in the sense of *malefici* and *venefici*.

This result came partly as a consequence of an apocalyptic interest within Christianity in the aftermath of the schism between the Eastern Orthodox and Western Catholic Churches. The theological debate was concerned with unity of God in a Church that could not find it within themselves. This led to a feeling of apocalyptic despair, the recurring theme in Christian iconography from the 12th Century, where the Final Judgement in all its sublime horror found its form.

It is in this time of change and turmoil we find the seeds of the image of Satan as a grotesque mimic of God's holiness. The Inquisition was soon to take form as a tool for cleansing the Church of its heresies.

Satan was a living reality for the clergy, the power of separation and adversity, the power that threatened to break God's unity. The passages in the Gospel of Matthew and in John's Apocalypse detailing this Mystery were subject for theological speculation and artistic renderings in Christian iconography. Here we find references to the separation of the goat's and the sheep, the right and the left hand. The Devil and his angels preside over Hell, understood as a fiery realm within the Earth.

The goat as representative of the Devil and his kingdom is evident in the 15th trump of the Tarot and in Eliphas Levi's famous depiction of Baphomet. This imagery surfaced in the witch trial confessions in central Europe toward the end of the 15th Century.[8] The modern segmentation of left and right hand path also owes something to this predominantly Christian classification.

This found its way to Brazil, where spirit work with Umbanda is divided into "workings on the right side" and "workings on the left side".

This form of segmentation has a long historical precedence. The historian Baroja tells of heretics in 13th Century Germany referring to themselves as Luciferians. They venerated a black cat, after which, the candles were extinguished and an orgiastic feast celebrated. When the candles were again lit a black or dark man was summoned to appear. This man was said to have a body that shone like the Sun, while his lower part was furry like a cat.[9]

Nigel Jackson recounts a similar theme in *Call of the Horned Piper*, where in Ashton-upon-Lyne the prosecuted was said to be "Riding the Black Lad", a spirit-form possessed of "burning eyes".

In the 12th Century we see the Devil depicted with cloven hoofs, horns and tail - a bestial mimic of the human form. The irony is that for the people adhering to the peasant Craft this form was strikingly similar to the Lord of wild nature, virility, death and sex. The goat as a representative of the Devil, with its notorious devilish eyes, strength, virility and strong smell is conjoined with the emerging image of Satan.

The whole idea of left or sinister is often distorted. In astrology a *sinister* movement of planetary bodies signifies a motion towards a position or aspect, while *dexter* signifies a movement away. A sinister movement warns of an influence about to emerge; whether it is a good or bad influence depends on the nature of the planet and the aspects.

Famously Hindu *Vama Marga* is the sinister path, while in reality the name denotes the position of women in the tantric *panchamakara* ritual. Dadaji Mahendranath, the Guru of the Nath succession in the East writes of this in his article "Sinistroversus":

"The other division in Tantrika is known as Vama Marga or Nivritti Marga. Vama means left or opposite-turning because Dakshin means normal, sun wise or clockwise. Vama is not a religion but a spiritual esoteric path for those who have the basic qualifications. It is the path of return, left-turning or sinistroversus. First it is the path of return to the natural life of natural relationships and therefore differs from the restraint patterns and rules required for the slaves. Slaves must serve and not enjoy; they must worship and not attain. Vama Marga is also known as Bhukti Mukti Karnika — The Path of Enjoyment and Liberation. The path is not for everyone. To escape from the world, the rounds of rebirth and the miseries of life requires a way whereby one tastes the Microcosm in all its aspects. Without this experience, one can hardly have the capacity to reject. This is the way of the Gods and the way of the Masters."

Another recurring theme in the descriptions of the Devil in the historical record is his "blackness". Richard Cavendish[10] recounts an episode from Orleans in 1022 where a group of heretics were executed for worshipping the Devil. The Devil first appeared to them as an Ethiopian, or black man, and later as an angel of light. We see here a caricature of the Satan-Lucifer theme.

In 1587 in Soissons, France, Catherine Darea beheaded two girls with a sickle – one of them her own daughter. She explained the act by saying that the Devil in the shape of a black man had appeared to her, given her the sickle and ordered the killings!

There are many interesting elements here, as it transmits the idea of the wild wood hiding divine illumination. This same idea is found in antiquity where the nymphs and muses of springs and woodlands also give illumination, insight and power in their mystic revelry of light. In the next chapter we shall look more in depth on these important elements of the Craft.

The wilderness, like the crossroad, has become firmly established as the dwelling of the Devil. In Romanticism it was the woodland deity Pan who became the recurring icon of the untamed powers. Pan was the Greek Lord of the wilderness, a guardian of shepherds, a muse for flute-players. His form was bestial, with horns and the lower part of the body in the form of a goat. He was the seducer of women and a great lover of nymphs.

Faunus, the Roman equivalent, was one of the *di indigetes* deities, meaning that he belonged to the oldest strata of Roman spirituality. As with so many other deities, he was also seen as a former divine king, known as Fatuus, related to fate, divination and prophecy.

It has been suggested that Faunus was actually the *Lupercus*, which ties him in with a rich ancestry of Romans as a people born from wolves. The spirit-herd attending Faunus was known as Fauns, nymph-like genius loci of the woodland, just like the satyrs attending Pan.

Similar themes occur in Fairy lore of Northern Europe. The fairies or Sidhe were said to have their habitat in woodlands. Legends and fairytales speak of a Queen to this otherworldly realm and also about a horned man with the serpent power that runs like a fire through the Earth – and in men. "Kundalini" is the same type of fire as the telluric fire ascribed to Old Nick. It is this fire that rises in the *volva* when she travels out by her ecstatic *seidr*, the word itself being a reference to the cooking fire.

Faunus is this serpentine fire that runs through the woodland and creates the prophetic upsurge along ley-lines. The Lord of Untamed Wilderness, given that he is the original Lupercus is reprised in the imagery of the twins suckled by a she wolf.

This wolf is either their mother or foster-mother Larenta, mother of Lares whose feast day was around the winter solstice. Latin *lupa* can mean both wolf as well as prostitute (*lupa* was a common slang for prostitutes in Roman times). She is also associated with Fauna, who had a shrine and an oracular priestess close to the Aventine Hills. As Fauna she was also given the names Luperca, Dea Dia and Bona Dea, a reference to the virginal daughter of Larenta and Faunus whose worship was by "wine and myrtle", clearly Venusian references.

The similarities between *Bona Dea* and the Sabine Goddess *Ops* suggests the combination of two Pagan deities perhaps a forced interchange between Roman legions and the Sabean women. The wilderness or the wild wood seem to be crucial here as it was exactly the women of the wild regions Romulus and his warrior band sought out to be the mothers of their children.

Lupercalia and Saturnalia contributed to the form, myth and function of the modern day witchcraft revivals. The festival of Lupercalia was originally held on the 15th February but was moved to the 1st February to coincide with Candelaria. Candelaria was celebrated in honour of St. Valentine, who lends his name to Valentine's day when frank expression of love and affection ward off malefic influences.

Varro states that Lupercalia was a pastoral festival older than the founding of Rome. The original purpose of Lupercalia was to purify the city and exorcise malignant spirits and hostile beings. Justin the Martyr identified Lupercus (i.e. he who wards off the wolf) with Faunus, giving the attributes of Pan as hailed by the poets of the Romantic era.

The Devil & the Trickster

The Devil is a notorious trickster. Many prefer the Jungian interpretation of this archetype. But Jung ignored the association of the archetypical with the world of 'Platonic forms'. He gave a distorted explanation, ripped from its original context and placed in the world of profane activity.

The term 'archetype' as used in the works of Plotinus was a reference to the ideas in the Divine Mind. We might say that archetypes are Platonic forms. Jung was referred to quite subjective structures related to the world below the Noetic sphere. The traditional distinctions are crucial if we are to understand the metaphysical meaning of the Art, something evident in the works of Henry Cornelius Agrippa.

Deities reputed to be trickster are Odin, Loki, Prometheus, Esu, Hermes, Set, Anansi, Aphrodite, Cupid and animals such as the fox, raven, coyote and others that share a nature of thievery and deception. The word trickery is derived from Old French, *trique,* meaning 'cheat' or 'deception'. This is probably from the Latin *tricae* that was used in a variety of circumstances. One meaning was 'to shuffle' and another referred to a 'tangle of difficulties'. The word was used in medieval France as well as in Latin to designate conditions related to games of chance, but the latter interpretation is also significant - it denotes the condition people find themselves in when they go to the crossroad. It is possible to combine the idea of life as a game and the tangled conditions with which we are at times confronted. The player who holds the dice in his hand is taking a chance. He is at the crossroad. The lovelorn woman consulting Exu is placing herself at the crossroad.

Typical tricksters possess wisdom and hidden knowledge, but they make access difficult. My informant on German Hexencraft tells me that followers of Odin often enjoy bad luck. There are other deities, like Prometheus who are more altruistic in their trickery.

The Devil is a trickster, but no bluffer at card games or senseless confuser. In many lineages of traditional witchcraft this condition is referred to as "being in exile" or subject to an ordeal or test where the conclusion is renewed knowledge and wisdom. It is the finding of light within the wilderness. In essence the situation is as follows; you come to the crossroad, entangled in confusion and you want direction. Or you come to the crossroad in search of wisdom only the "Devil" can give. As such the more potent example of the journey through the crossroads is found in the myths and imagery of Odin and of Cain, two carriers of the witch blood that earned their deification by the path of ordeal.

If we turn to Hermes as guardian of doors, gateways, merchants, alchemists and thieves – the recurring theme is the one of change, opportunity and fluidity. The role of the trickster is typified by the spirit and temperament of the planet Mercury. Crucially for an understanding of Mercury, according to traditional sources such as William Lilly, this planet takes on the properties of whatever stellar body to which it is conjoined. This means that he is good with good and ill with ill, male with male and female with female. Mercury is considered cold, dry and melancholic and is said to rule the spirits of animals.

Odin is depicted in this exact form. Odin alone is cold, dry and melancholic, but with his mistress Freya he blossoms, just as Mercury blossoms in conjunction with Venus. Following Lilly we find that animals under his domain are the hyena, ape, fox, squirrel, serpent and spider. He is reputed to be the vehicle for divination. His herbs are vervain, anis and dragonworth and especially nut trees. In Islamic lore nut trees are seen as dangerous places, the reputed resting place of djinns.

Ordeal, trickery and chance can be tools to stimulate our growth. Odin sacrificed himself to himself on the axis mundi to gain the wisdom and understanding just as the Lord Cain was exiled, by God. If we embrace the challenge of the crossroad we will be rewarded with a clear understanding of our mission, purpose and destiny.

It is this that meets us when we venture to the crossroad to commune with the Devil in his many guises and masks. The Devil will come and open the game of chance. Choose and take the consequences. We have the dictum used in the Craft, 'May the Curse, Cunning and Blessing be' —

The Horns of the Devil

The Devil has horns — but so does Michelangelo's Moses. It has been commonly accepted that the horns refer to the Moon.

Cernunnos or Karneios is a horned deity, whose name shares the root KRN which gives rise to words meaning 'power' and 'elevation'.

CARTARI-JANUS DEPICTED IN
RELATION TO KRONOS

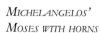

MICHELANGELOS'
MOSES WITH HORNS

The same root KRN is also found in Kronos. This is a link with Saturn as the power of elevation. The same root, 'KRN' gives us the words 'cornus' and 'corona' and 'karneios'. We see here a relationship between horns (cornus), crown (corona) and power (karneios). Karneios-Karn means 'high place' as a symbol of the Pole and the sacred mountain, a term also used to describe the pile of stones (cairn) a tumulus or tomb.

The Land of the Gods becomes the Land of the Dead when the spiritual centre disappears, which explains the transition of Kronos as a God of the evershining Golden Age to the Lord of Death. We see here the life giving and death dealing attribute of this power signified by the horns.

Following this thread the Devil's trident is like Siva's trident (trishula), and denote supremacy and ascent to the summit. Note also the similarity between the thorn and the horn, thorns on the crown denoting multiple insights.

The Greek word Keraunos, meaning 'thunderbolt' derives from the same root and we see an interesting theme surfacing related to horns or crown - for it is at the summit the lightning is most likely to strike. Moses with his horns may represent a lunar balance and power as well as a direct reference to luminous rays of the mountain. We cannot escape the significance of Alexander the Great, the son of horned God Amun. Rene Guénon points out that horns can both denote solar and lunar power, the ram of Amun being solar and the bull being predominantly lunar. Commonly the two horns were seen as dexter and sinister, east and west.

In the Greco-Roman world there was no agreed opinion on the nature of magic. There was a distinction between harmful and not harmful. We shall use *Megas Alexandros* as our 'icon' to symbolize this period of cultural transition regarding the understanding of magic and witchcraft, because it is in the form of Alexander we find the arts coming together.

He was born in July 356 BC and died in 323 BC in Babylon. His name in Aramaic and Arabic is particularly interesting for our study. In Aramaic it was *Tre-Qarnayia,* and in Arabic *Dhul-Qarnayn,* meaning two horned. And here we find one of the earliest influences on the 'Horned Master of the Craft' in Wicca and witchcraft.

He is considered by historians to be the meeting point between Greek and non-Greek cultures, friendly towards migration and cultural exchange. Through his teacher Aristotle he developed a taste for philosophy, including "the liberal arts". He was a hero, his lineage stretching back to Achilles on his mother's side and to Heracles on his father's. He was the birth son of King Philip and his fourth wife, Olympias, who was reputed to sleep in a bed of snakes!

Olympias had a dream where a spirit came and sealed her with the image of a lion. She went to a seer who interpreted this to mean that the child would have this characteristic. The temple of Artemis in Ephesus burned down the night Alexander was born. When still a young man he went to the Oracle of Ammon at Siwa which revealed that Alexander's father was none other than Zeus.

In Alexander's time Ammon was considered a major deity, a mixture of Ra and Horus, with features similar to Sol Invictus, and even the cult of Mithras cultivated by the Roman soldiers. The Egyptian heritage entered Europe through Alexander.

The Egyptian connection was strong, not only with Alexander, but also Julius Gaius Caesar. The classical threefold segmentation is into Heaven,

Earth and the Underworld. With Ptolemy the geo-centric worldview entered the world. The Ptolemaic worldview was one of organic and natural interaction, a holistic connectedness where the formlessness of the beginning separated itself into Heaven and Earth as representing mother and father.

The Earth as the centre of the Cosmos was marked by sacred mountains hence the Gods lived on Olympus, the *omphalos* or navel of the world. This cosmic center designated the importance of the four cardinal points and the idea of the axis mundi that linked the zenith and nadir of the cosmic realm, creating a perfect geometrical cosmic harmony. Mankind needed to be in a 'geometric' proximity with the Gods in order to enjoy the nutrition and protection of the divine.

In Ptolemy we find Babylonian and Egyptian astronomy and astrology meeting each other in the richness of Greek thinking. Of this holistic and geocentric worldview Martin has the following to say:

> "*From a geocentric perspective, the Moon was the closest of the planets to the Earth, and Saturn the most distant. Mercury, Venus, Sun, Mars and Jupiter occupied positions two, three, four, five and six respectively. The terrestrial, sub-lunar realm was sharply separated from the celestial super-lunar realm by an abyss of cosmic space populated by elemental and demonic powers. These powers controlled the terrestrial realm, even as they in turn were controlled by the celestial deities…at the same time, an earlier chthonic (from the Greek* chthon *meaning Earth; of the Underworld and its spirits) evocation of sacrality began to flourish in place of the relocated celestial sacrality. The ancient festival of Demeter, Goddess of grain, celebrated at Eleusis, enjoyed renewed popularity in the Hellenistic world and survived well into the period of Roman decline; and the orgiastic frenzies of Dionysus, the very embodiment of chthonic spirit, swept the Hellenistic world*". (Martin; 1987: 7,8)

Roman religion was based upon absorbing neighbouring cults and Gods. This was so, in particular with the Sabine and Etruscan deities, while Celtic deities were recognized as wilder manifestations of the Roman deities.

It has been suggested that Janus was the very same as the Etruscan Culsans, a deity of doors and doorways. Culsans had a female consort, Culsu, who presided over the same domains, but was particularly related to the Underworld. Her emblems were the scissors and torch suggesting a relationship with Hecate and Diana. She was the dominatrix of the crossroad similar to Fortuna, with her wheel and scissors, presided over Fate.

Fortuna and Diana were cults imported by the Etruscan king Tullius. Reading the accounts, historically and scholarly, one gets the idea that Romans were not necessarily preoccupied with their own deities' superiority. Culsu became dislocated from Culsans as he assimilated with Janus. The necromantic aspects of Culsans were taken over by Greek Hecate; prophecy and Fate by Fortuna.

Emerging from this we have the necromantic and oracular elements, the relation with Fate - needed if the oracles are to be useful. The role of Janus is important for the understanding of witchcraft. Originally Janus was depicted with one half of his face shaven and the other bearded, holding a key. This iconography reminds me of Basque Janicot, where the Sun and the Moon are the eyes.

The nymph Carna aids Janus to control the timelines. As a reward he gives Carna dominion of door hinges, the possibility of turning time back and forth.

The historical episode of Romulus' men kidnapping the gothic or Sabine women recall how Janus caused a hot spring to gush forth and thus hinder the attack. It is interesting to note Janus' relationship with fire, springs and nymphs. Hermes took on some qualities of Janus, while Janus himself followed a quite different development, turning more like Pan. Culsans is remembered as Jack in the Wood, Robin Goodfellow and similar myths. He was a lover of nymphs represented by the serpentine fire of the woodlands. On a mystical level it shows the importance of Hermes in magic and witchcraft from the Middle Ages and in particular during the Renaissance. The wise art is related to the woodlands and the kingdom of Faunus. It is the untamed Gods and spirits, trickery, possibility, the powers of frustration and radical change found in the undiluted and pagan (as opposed to civilized) order that is the home of the Craft.

The Keys to the Kingdom

The motif of reversal is found in the crucifixion of St. Peter. Origen commented that Peter felt that he should not be crucified in the same way as the master and should be hanged upside down as a sign of his unworthy state. The inverted cross with two keys is a symbol that hearkens back to Janus; the Lord of past and present who holds the keys to the celestial spheres and the realm of the netherworld. In Christian theology the symbolism of the keys is related to judgement day. St. Peter meets one after death and opens the doors to Jerusalem, Heaven or Purgatory.

Pope John Paul the II evoked accusations of Satanism when in a visit to Israel he wore vestments displaying an inverted cross. In the mid 1800s Eugene Vintras, founder of the Church of Carmel was accused of witchcraft and diabolism, because of the many miracles he performed and also because of a similar vestment. For Vintras this was a symbol of humility, but the connections to Abbe Boullan (who was excommunicated from Vintras' congregation) intensified the diabolic rumours. Boullan became infamous for his sex magic workings with the nun Chevalier, aimed at the birth of a perfect child.

CARAVAGGIO'S CRUCIFIXION OF ST. PETER (1601)

Vintras' visions and work with the inverted cross, made it a symbol quite contrary to its original usage. Vintras was preoccupied with love, mercy and grace and claimed that these powers caused the miracle of his bleeding hosts that appeared during his Mariavite masses.

Aleister Crowley commented that the inverted cross signified a falling away from the Lord's mercy and grace. Anton La Vey, the founder of the Church of Satan saw in the inverted cross the reversal of Christendom and thus a sign of power on earth and a deliberate rejection of the promise of heavenly perfection in the afterlife.

The "satanic" interpretation is both erroneous and misguided, another example of how symbols can be emptied of their traditional meaning to be invested with something completely alien. For example the Third Reich's usurped the swastika and certain runes and gave it a meaning contrary to its original mystery. However, St. Peter was the one entrusted with the keys, just as Kronos entrusted them to Janus.

A SHIELD WITH ST. PETERS CROSS AND KEYS

A Call to the Powers of the Crossroad

He stands at the crossroad, with horn and stang, awaiting the toll of the bell and the foot of those sworn to the exile that ends in the grave and tears. By many names he has been called and to retain the mask we shall refer to him as Devil or he who carries the horns. The horns of Selene, the horns of juxtaposition, the horns of one and the other, the horns that mark transition – the sanctity of murder and rebellion.

He is the glory of the Light and the path of the ascending power. Be no fool as you seek to take the power, in the blink of an eye, the power that turns, turns. Towards and against, like the tide, amongst his own. Simple is the power. And for this purpose this ritual is presented as a diminutive beacon illuminating the points of the crossroad, a breach in the texture of night, a whisper amongst the forgotten legions.

So take thy candle, be it red, black or green and place upon thy shrine the icon of the Devil. Take the garland of roses and number thy prayers 7 & 70 for the perfection of the prophets.

Know that black holds the riddle of night, red the riddle of blood and green the riddle of land.

And for the beads, take wood, pearl or bone. Pilgrim, walk across the ladder and stray not on thy journey. For a lovelorn stranger falls into the siren's embrace and seduction and misery will be the crossroad's gift. With secure step and thy hand fast, thy heart should be fast and secure on the path of faith. So, in front of the candle pray as follows:

Intercessor at the crossroad of the Earth

Lover of the Toad faced obsessors in the gardens of Night

Lord of the many cities of exile

Master of the Horse and Stang

Oath taker, oath-breaker

Master of opportunity

The hand that turns the wheel

Instigator of the screams heard through the adamantine desert of our all aloneness

Flaming Lord of Earth and forge

You who art iron and gold

You who art Devil and Saint

Meet us at the crossroad of rebellion

Meet us at the port of besiegement

Hand down the key to the tower of enemies' destruction

And lend their tongue to the sweetness of Fortune

We call thee from the heart of the True Cross

As the children of exile

Thy brood and bane be upon our brow

Lend us thy helping hand as we search the secrets of murder

Help us in the pursuit of understanding

Help us as you unleash the secret powers

Against our oppressors, strike hard

Against our oppressing fall, strike hard

May my heart be cleansed by thy fire

Leave only the pure soul back to walk the serene path of the master

And if I have been found wanting in my demand

Strike me without mercy

May the curse set aflame all corners of my life

Until cunning descends

For the sake of my soul there is no thing or no one

I will not forswear

For the pursuit of wisdom there is no path I will leave un-tread

For you hold the key to the kingdoms of high and low

You are the man robed in gold and night at the ladders of light

You are the naked youth at the ladders of hell

You are the height and depth and the point between

Father, Saint, Devil and Master

Such is our petition

So mote it be, now and forever more

From height to depth, from dextral to sinister

We call upon thee to meet us in the crossroad of power

Take now thy rose garland in thy hand and solemnly pray by each step taken:

Oh Holy St. Peter, Lord of the Key, Lord of the Gate, The Stone of Wisdom

Grant me the key and open the door. Follow me on the Dragon's Road.

So mote it be.

Amen

By the 77th prayer said to the praise of the crossroad you will kiss the cross and say:

Father, Saint, Devil and Master

From the True Cross

May Our prayers be heard

To the True Cross

All Powers will descend

For such is my petition

And such is my prayer

As good Saint Peter is my fellow journeyman

Amen

Dama de Elphame - Audrey Melo

3

The Blood of the Living Bones

Kāna I-insānu hayyatan fil-qidam
"Formerly man was a serpent"

The ancestry and nature of the witches has been vividly debated. Can anyone become a witch by rites of ingress or is the witch born. Does the "witchblood" refer to a specific genetic, spiritual descent - or daimonic intervention?

Every year on the 8th of April the Gypsies celebrate the day of their ancestors Qayin and Calmena. In recent times there has been a renewed interest in the Merovingian bloodline, the so-called Graal (signifying womb) line.

From the 10th Century mystical Mosaic traditions spoke of a decent from celestial vipers. In the Garden of Eden the serpent is said to commune with the first couple and mate with the Lilith and Cheva.

The idea of the Fall is not unique to the Western mystery traditions; we find similar themes on the African continent. Yoruba myths tell how Osanyin, the Lord of herbs, fell from the sky and sunk into the earth in the city Iràwò. The name of the city means 'star'. Oduduwa, the founder of Ile Ife ('City of Love'), the sacred city of the Yoruba is said to have fallen from the heavens. Other myths say he came from Mecca, or from Egypt and yet others that he fell from the heavens. Oduduwa had sixteen sons and these founded kingdoms on the West African coast. Today, traditional kingdoms still trace their lineage back to Oduduwa.

In Yoruba/Ifá metaphysics we are all divine beings going through a human incarnation. Likewise, the Dogons of Mali, the Fon of Benin, the Ewe of Congo, the Yoruba and Hausa of Nigeria, the Vodusaints of Haiti and several mystical traditions related to the great monotheist religions of the world claim a similar heritage.

It is said that these beings lived in harmony with all those on Earth, until they were touched with supernatural powers and became destructive. The ruler of heaven allowed the waters to rise and most of the Eniyan died, and it is from this line comes the witch-blood.

I suggest that this light seed, that is often referred to as 'witch blood' went through Cain and Seth, Abel's replacement. The "Mark of Cain" was given by God. Seth was marked by this light seed because in him nothing was corrupt. In Seth we find the royal and sacerdotal initiation conferred by God himself and thus Seth is the unity his name expresses.

In numerology his name totals 700, the same value of the Hebrew letter *nun* also sacred to *Akrav,* the Scorpion, a great protector of sages and wonderfully wise in its own right. The *Akrav* is also the protector of the Rav or Master who ventures within the fields of *Keshuph*. This nomadic sorcery of the Hebrews aims at re-integration and restitution of corruption. Likewise *Shath*, meaning pillar and prince; and *Kapporeth* the Mercy Seat all add up to 700.

Witches have long been associated with scorpions, owls, crows, toads, serpents and dragons. These animals commonly inspire fear or/and fascination, because of the otherworldly cunning these animals possess.

Nichoals de Vere claimed to be a living descendant of such elven blood, the dragon kings and queens that habited the Earth and originated the bloodline of the Merovingians that flowed through men like King Arthur, son of Utter Pendragon. In his book *The Dragon Legacy* de Vere's raises several interesting points, perhaps obscured by his preoccupation with proving his own genealogical descent. He opines that mankind is not equal and that this is a modern idea, based on a misguided democratic notion that everyone can be whatever they choose. His ideas are completely in agreement with some versions of the *via sacra* tradition.

The Hermetic axiom, "As above, so below", means that we need to realize and expand upon our station in life and destiny. We need to find our place, which may not be the place we actually want. A disorderly placement above will only give disorder below.

De Vere's presentation of his bloodline corresponds with myths all over the world of draconian or serpentine influences creating a bloodline. These themes are found in the Middle Eastern and European heritage, but also in African and South American legends. They tell of an outlandish race ascending to the mountain or to the top of trees to escape catastrophe. What we understand to be witch blood is just one of many ways of expressing this particular pedigree. The blood of this race touches those who are truly witches, so rites of ingress serve to quicken the seed already there.

> *De Vere says:*
>
> *"The word 'dragon" is derived from the Greek 'edrakon', which is an aorist of the word 'derkesthai' " mesninh 'to see clearly'. The Dragon is the inherited Dragon as archetype and that archetype is the conduit of clear sight through which racial knowledge flows. Clear sight also and principally refers to transcendent consciousness."*

This blood passed through aristocracies, so for example the *Lemegeton* is arranged in accordance with the aristocratic dignity, dukes, earls, princes and so forth. We might refer to this as the royal witchblood, while a people like the Gypsies possess a blood of a different making, it is still witchblood. The blood descending from Seth carries a sacerdotal quality, whilst the blood of Cain transmits the regal fire. A seed is just a seed and if it does not receive nutrition and attention it will not sprout. Likewise, if it is planted in a corrupt culture it will not prosper or will grow into a deformed hybrid. The bloodline imparts a special sensibility and power to witches. This means that even today witchblood is transmitted by faeric intervention.

The Royal blood of Angels

The particular blood that ignites wisdom speaks of angelic origin, it is star blood. Angels are often involved in the birth of unique individuals. Jesus Christ's birth was heralded by an Angel of the Lord who carried the particular seed. Over the last decades we have witnessed a growing interest in the star blood of Lucifer. The Luciferian motif has been with us for at least 1000 years, but in the Craft, Madeline Montalban and her Order of the Morningstar should be noted. Montalban introduced the name Lumiel, rather than Lucifer and saw him as the angel of Earth and mankind's protector. The same angelic power also surfaced in the works of the British witch, Andrew Chumbley.

Michael Howard, a student of Montalban in the book, *The Pillars of Tubal Cain*, co-authored with Nigel Jackson, provides the following attributes and domains to Lumiel. He is an ageless man in a shining white robe, a blazing white star on his brow, his neck adorned with a silver Tau cross entwined with a serpent. He is considered to be an angel, with a preference for teaching women. He is a source of help when all else fails. His colour is said to be violet and his stones are emerald and crystal.

Deities that possess similar traits are Osiris, Ptah, Adonis, Tammuz, Attis, Mithra, Balder, Lugh, Dionysus, Pan, Krishna and Christ. All these deities are related to sacrifice. Of these we might say that it is the Mysteries of Osiris - Tammuz -Mithra - Dionysus - Christ that depicts Lumiel's essence as we see the celestial descent and terrestrial sacrifice. It is through such descent that the Archangel of Earth was set to watch and illuminate the world.

Several Craft myths set great importance on the account in the sixth chapter of *Genesis,* which speaks of the fall of the watchers. The accounts of the fall in the first chapter of *The Book of Enoch* define more clearly the nature of the fall. In 1667 the cleric and historian Daniel Defoe summarize the angelic corruption in an interesting way in his history of the black arts:

'But tho' he suffer'd Martyrdom for his Scheme (having been expell'd the Parliament of two Kingdoms for it) we do not find he has yet had the Benefit of his Project, so we must wait till he is pleased to make the Experiment. But to return to the Antediluveans: The old World, I say, as wicked as they were, had some shadow of Good in them, and for some Years, nay some hundreds of Years, they maintain'd the Character of the Sons of God, before they were debauched by the Daughters of Men; that is to say, before they blended the Race with the corrupt Seed of Cain, and mingled Blood with Idolaters. Where, by the way, we have an accurate Description of the Times, I mean in those early Days, of the Race; 'tis evident 'twas just then as 'tis now, the Ladies were the Devils of the Age; the Beauties, the Toasts, the fine Faces were the Baits; the Hell lay concealed in the Smiles of the charming Sex, They were the Magicians, taking the Word in its present Acceptation and its grossest Sense:

There lay the Witchcraft, and its Force was so irresistible, that it drew in even the Sons of God."

Similarly, we find in several European Craft myths the same basic themes. Related witch-lore is found amongst practitioners of Italian Craft or Stregoneria, in Leland's *Gospel of Aradia* and Paul Huson's *Mastering Witchcraft*. In the beginning was a vast darkness, whereupon Diana divides herself to create night and day. She retains rulership of night and gives the day to her brother, Lucifer, the Sun. Diana, in the form of a cat, i.e. behaving seductively like a cat, seduces her brother and gives birth to Herodias.

The same motif is seen in the interaction between Mesopotamian Na'amah, the seductress and Azael, which repeats an even earlier myth of Lilith's seduction of Schamash. Schamash the Sun in the kingdom of night, was given the fire and used this to ignite his blacksmith's forge. The Na'amah / Azael relation reveals the consequences of the seduction for the Sun and the womb. We see the same basic idea expressed in the tension between Tubal Qayin and Na'amah - the root of the fall and redemption. It was Na'amah that caused the fall.

There are many explanations as to the nature of this legendary fall - often moralistic or sentimental. Dionysus the Areopagite in his *Celestial Hierarchy* related the fall to sober observation concerning hierarchy or harmony:

> *"Hierarchy is, in my opinion, a holy order and knowledge and activity which, so far as is attainable, participates in the Divine Likeness, and is lifted up to the illuminations given it from God."[11]*

I suggest that the fall is simply a dislocation from the spiritual centre.

Losing sight of the vibrant centre causes a disruption in the established harmony, meaning that the fall of the watchers were simply a movement away from their harmonious station. The fall ignited in humans a thwarted, corrupt seed, born from their angelic father's misplaced desire.

The angels fell from a completely different order, not an inferior and terrestrial moral order. In Genesis 6:11 the Hebrew word used to denote the corrupted seed is from the root *shachath*, meaning 'decadence', 'destruction' and 'damage'. It is the same root as *chamath*, meaning 'crime', that is also used in the 6th chapter of Genesis to denote corrupted ways. There is an explicit sexual connotation here related to perversion the violation of women.

Genesis says that the *Nefilims* took whom they wanted of women. The commentary on the Torah, *Yalkuth Me'am Lo'ez*, edited by the late Aryeh Kaplan points out that the word *Nefilim* can also be written *Nefalim* meaning 'aborted infant'. It was common amongst the Hebrews to give herbal philtres to provoke abortions in cases where the woman had suffered rape or become pregnant with the child of a man other than her husband.

Rabbinical doctrine suggested that mere fantasizing of another during coitus would bring the qualities of that person into the child. The *Nefilim* was reputed to be stunningly beautiful and capable of provoking lust and erotic thoughts in the mind and heart of women. This may be the reason why the *Nefilim* were called *Anshey Shem*, 'Renowned names'.

The *Nefilim* were called by several names; *Eymim*, which refers to fear. They are also *Refa'im*, because their voices made the heart turn to wax. They were also Gibborim and Zamzumim, because of their strong physique and readiness for battle.

Anakim, from *Anak*, the Sun and thus related to the solar eclipse as they overshadowed the light from the unmovable mover, the pole of righteousness. And they were also, *Avvim*, a word borrowed from Aramaic, meaning simply 'a snake' in the sense of 'something that lives in the dust'.

The Talmud tells of an Arab who travelled with Rabbi Chana in the desert and who navigated back to civilization by smelling and tasting the sand. Some of the angelic and serpentine seed became corrupt and this provoked the flood. Noah went into the ark with his wife Na'amah. There was another race of men in whom the seed had not become corrupted, that went to Mount Hermon and Sinai. This was the race of Seth, Adam's third son. We shall look at this more closely in the 4th Chapter.

The origin of the witch blood is related to the fall. Let us again return to the *Celestial Hierarchy* and the nature of the third order of angels, the Thrones, from whence the fall occurred.

> *"In the third rank are those who, from their unity, simplicity, constancy and firmness, are sometimes called Thrones, sometimes Seats; who themselves also are wise and loving. But from their simplicity, they have the attributes of unity, power, strength, fortitude, and steadfastness. Which very attributes the Cherubim and Seraphim also possess... Steadfastness comes from simplicity, simplicity from purification. For when each object is purified back to its own simple nature, then, being un-compounded, it remains indissoluble through its unity. Whence it is clear that purification is assigned to the Thrones. Moreover, when a thing is purified, it is illumined, and after it is illumined, it is perfected. This last office is given to the Seraphs, the other to the Cherubs."[12]*

Speaking of the third order of angels, we see a faint echo of the importance of the number three in fairytales and witchcraft myths, new and old. This third order of angels, have a specific correlation to the third heaven, the *Shehaqim,* and it is here the secrets of the fall is found.

The third heaven is described in the *Second Book of Enoch* (also called *Book of the Secrets of Enoch*) as being the original location of the Garden of Eden. Here we find the Tree of Life. It is a curious heaven, *Shehaqim* has a dual quality. To the north is the gate to the hell where sodomites, witches, sorcerers and other people that commit 'sin against nature' are sent. It is also reputed to be the crossroad between corruption and incorruptibility.

The third heaven is a geometric outline of the original paradise. Hell is in the north, one of the epithets of Lilith is 'The Northern One'. Islamic angelology says that Jibrail took Mohammad to this heaven and showed him paradise. Cain was exiled to the north. Rabbinical commentators say Anahael has dominion here and Christian mystics say this is the heaven of Azrael.

The topography of the third heaven allows us to understand the very nature of the Garden of Eden. In this heaven we find the angelic origins of the witch blood. This is presented in the following passage from 2 Enoch, a Slavic manuscript that was probably translated from a lost Greek original.

> *VIII.* Of the assumption of Enoch to the third heaven.
>
> *AND those men took me thence, and led me up on to the third heaven, and placed me there; and I looked downwards, and saw the produce of these places, such as have never been known for goodness.*
>
> *2 And I saw all the sweet-flowering trees and beheld their fruits, which were sweet-smelling, and all the foods borne by* them *bubbling with fragrant exhalation.*
>
> *3 And in the midst of the trees that of life, in that place whereon the Lord*

rests, when he goes up into paradise; and this tree is of ineffable goodness and fragrance, and adorned more than every existing thing; and on all sides it is in form gold-looking and vermilion and fire-like and covers all, and it has produce from all fruits.

4 Its root is in the garden at the earth's end.

5 And paradise is between corruptibility and incorruptibility.

6 And two springs come out which send forth honey and milk, and their springs send forth oil and wine, and they separate into four parts, and go round with quiet course, and go down into the PARADISE OF EDEN, between corruptibility and in corruptibility.

7 And thence they go forth along the earth, and have a revolution to their circle even as other elements.

8 And here there is no unfruitful tree, and every place is blessed.

The Blood from the Other Side

Through the earth and the land, through veins and subterranean streams runs the blood of our ancestors. The land is in our blood. From humans, through animals and reptiles - their roots stretch deep down within the cave of memory where they nurture wisdom on the bones of our ancestors.

The knowledge of our ancestors was communicated to Odin, the man-god of Scandinavia, who received the Runes in his act of self-sacrifice to himself. By this act he went down within the arcane memory of Gods and men to retrieve wisdom. Our familiars, be they dog or toad, bird or snake, cat or boar, are living witness to our ancestry, our kinship with nature, our stream of blood stretching through time.

The idea that witches are descendants from a different race ties in with the witch as someone who refuses to conform. The spirit of rebellion lies at the core of his or her nature. She prefers the wild and unrestrained outdoors to the isolated dusty urban conclaves of human life. She is a child of nature marked and viewed as something other.

From North to South we find legends and Fairy tales about spirits from the other side taking the shape of comely men and women to seduce mortals. The offspring of these unions would have a foot in each world and when they hear the call from Anwynn they remain in the realm of death.

The Boto seducing a fair maiden by Regiane Bassani

In Amazonia we have legends of the Boto, a pink dolphin that lives in the sweet waters. On moonlight nights this dolphin can take the shape of a handsome man to seduce - or rape - women to generate children. We see here similarities with the *Nephilim*. Similarly the mermen have an aggressive reputation as seducers.

This peculiar pedigree will naturally create a yearning for something lost. For the witch the land itself is a constant reminder of life and death as an eternal cycle. The other side is spoken of as a flight, a crossing of a river, or opening of the doors of the castle or a feeding of the land. We are the living link in a vast cyclical chain of being and by reconnecting with the mighty deeds of the witches of the land will enflame our blood anew.

The trafficking with the other side, with the denizens of Elphame, before the coming of modernity was much more common. Elias Ashmole (1617 – 1692), the founder of the Royal Society, was a diligent astrologer, a Rosicrucian and the first man to present an account of initiation into Accepted Freemasonry. He grew up with a deep resonance with the marshlands of Lichfield and the little parish church reputed to host the bones of St. Chad, patron of madmen.

The moors themselves were in the 13th Century frequently referred to as the fields of the dead. Ashmole encountered beings from the Fairy realm, nymphs dancing on the moorlands and around springs. He was marked by the spirit presences such as the piper with eyes "out of the ordinary" that imparted hidden knowledge to the young Elias Ashmole. As Tobias Churton[13] comments:

> *"Ashmole's mature philosophy certainly held room for the secret life of these supposed strange, intermediate being. It was customary to give fayrie-like characteristics to the spirits of the elements: of earth,* gnomes; *of water,* undines; *of air,* sylphs; *and of fire,* salamanders. A Midsummer Night's Dream *and* The Tempest *were modern plays when Ashmole was a boy.*

But whereas the four traditional elements were everywhere and constituted everything, the "fayries" were quite particular about their chosen place. Not every house was suitable for fairies. It was a question of location, *of* locus, *of* genius loci, *and of* locus genii. *Ashmole could hardly have been a stranger to the concept of magic of place, whether that magic induced ecstasy or* panic.

Ashmole represented the typical cunning man of his time. He was a learned man who related to Elphame or "the other side". He maintained a heathen philosophy and simultaneously venerated the Church and the Christian Mysteries. Congress with fairies was veiled by taboos. Cunning people who were reputed to gain their gifts from fairies would not divulge anything regarding "the other side".

Katharine Briggs and Emma Wilby point out the ease with which Irish peasants engaged in a dual faith. At this time it was quite common to see the Devil as the God of Earth and Jehovah as the God of Heaven. The relationship between them was dynamic and workable.

We tend to look at the past with a modern gaze and believe that theology and faith were as structured and accessible for our ancestors as it is for us. The coexistence of mutually exclusive principles was self-evident and not something that needed much analysis.

Elias Ashmole was marked by this world view, and well aware of the work of John Dee, Cornelius Agrippa and Iohannes Weyer. Men had an appetite for the Mysteries, letting the Divine Mind fill their souls. They were focused on unification and not much occupied with creating labels and boxes for the mystical and religious experience, as seen in contemporary occultism.

Let us take one dogma, widespread amongst present day Pagans, and derived from pseudo-academic studies of Margaret Murray and the creative romanticism of Gerald Gardner - The Old Faith or Old Religion is a Goddess cult.

When people of early modern Europe referred the "auld ffayth", they meant Roman Catholicism.[14] In spite of the English abolition of the Catholic faith in 1530 there were still a large number of people who retained beliefs and rituals concerning the saints, the cult of the dead and pilgrimages to sacred wells and springs. It is as though with Protestantism there was a 'romanization' of the old faith.

There is a curious text we shall bring forth at this point, Robert Kirk and his little monograph *The Secret Commonwealth,* originally written in 1691 but not published until 1893. Kirk was a minister and seventh son of a minister. He believed that the seventh child benefited from extraordinary spiritual gifts. It was said that Kirk was able to heal severe afflictions by touch.

So we see how a man of faith was engaged in dual observance, recognizing the reality of fairies and of Jehova. The existence of a hidden realm of spirits not associated with God's kingdom, ran the risk of denomination by the empire of Satan. Kirk's view is similar to that of Elias Ashmole. Andrew Lang who commented on Kirk's booklet suggests, that the land of Fairies merged with the ideas of Purgatory. After the Reformation the land of Fairies became less accessible to the people. This understanding fits with the myths of Anwynn as a subterranean kingdom evoking Hades, Hel and the castle in Robert Cochrane's vision, only accessible after crossing the river to the 'other side'.

Kirk presents a wealth of valuable information that can help us to understand Fairy lore. We see from Kirk's accounts that storytelling or fairytales were a vehicle for the preservation of the Mysteries. Those engaged in telling fairytales and stories concerning the dead could be viewed as witches. Scottish Archbishop Sharp was accused of entertaining "the muckle black Devil" in his study at midnight, and of being "levitated" and dancing in the air. These acts of levitation and spirit congress were also ascribed to the Neo-Platonists, in particular Plotinus. Even if Kirk tried to present a distinction between the Fairy domain and witchcraft it was fused with a practice belonging to the satanic Sabbath. Kirk resided in the Scottish highlands at Aberfoyle, an area with rich Celtic roots. There is a hill in Aberfoyle close to his church, where the fairies were said to dwell.

In many parts of Scotland it was considered crucial to build churches close to Fairy hills in order to ease the transition to the other side. Early folklorists commented these areas were reputed to house a subterranean people known as "Feens". We might have a common source for "fiend" and "Fairy" from this term. The rather out of fashion folklorist MacRitchie understood them to be the original Picts, described as a weird dwarfish race. He suggested that it was from encounters with these people that the Fairy beliefs originated.

The Realm of the Fairy Queen

I think it is fair to assume that Fairy beliefs are universal and legends about beings and settlements hidden from the gaze of ordinary sight are found in the mythical heritage of most cultures. But, in order to keep within the historical thread let us call forth the observations of Chaucer, who refers to Proserpina as the Fairy Queen. Proserpina, the Roman equivalent of Persephone means 'to emerge' and the myth tells of how she was playing with the nymphs, picking flowers when Pluto came out of the volcano Etna with four black horses to seduce or abduct her. Venus sent Cupid to Pluto in order to engender love in his heart and kingdom. As a result Pluto took Proserpina as his queen in Hades.

In order to rescue her, her mother Ceres annihilated the fertility of the Earth. Hermes intervened, an agreement was made and fertility restored. Proserpina's position is ambiguous. As Queen of the Underworld she possess the power to destroy. Here is a theme that goes back to the epic of Gilgamesh, with Inanna journeying to the throne of Ereshkigal, or Orpheus rescuing his beloved from the realm of death; or the Scottish ballad of Tamlane or Tam Lin abducted by the Fairies.

In all are found encounters with otherworldly beings. We have Orpheus with his nymphs, Tamlane with her Fairies and Proserpina with the Nereids as intercessors, friends or guides. These Fairy beings take on the properties of the dominant nature e.g. in the woods they are terrestrial.

There is also the abuse, as the Nereids abduct fair and mortal women to dance and make merry until they die of exhaustion. In accounts from all over the world the Fairies fall in love with mortals and engage in sexual relations. For Kirk, these subterranean people are departed souls. Like the lares and larvaes of the Romans, the genius of the wise ones and the familiar spirits of the witches, they are succubi, incubi or animals.

Kirk says that the Fairies or *Siths*, also known as *Sleagh Maith* or the Good People, commonly appear as a cloudy texture and that they are benevolent when they are given due respect and attention. This is similar to the woodland spirits of the Romans and the *Bona Dea*. In North Europe these beings are the 'Good Folk', 'The Good Lady' or the 'Good Ones'.

Kirk saw them as a mixture of man and angel. The ancients called them daemons, intelligent spirits with changeable bodies. They are reputed to be more visible in twilight although to see them one needs the second sight. They appear at funerals where they partake of the banquette, feeding on the essence of the food. It is interesting to note the connection with funerals. Kirk insists on a separation between the spirits used by witches and those that for him have a benevolent nature. Lang suggests Kirk lost his mind and common sense trying to explain these differences. He believed witches were in liaison with ambiguous spirits. The spirits, commonly understood to be familiars, were hostile, feeding upon fear, melancholy and pain and associated with foul or strong smells and the north. There is an antipathy between the powers of the north and those of the fair folk. Iron and loadstone, being items naturally drawn to the north, are the means of manifesting these ambiguous powers. Hence we find the belief that iron nails driven into the ground will drive away the 'good people', a subtle reference to the Cainite mythos and the first blacksmith and carrier of witch blood. This seed goes counter to the natural flow and order.

Kirk refers to these ambiguous spirits as 'Divels conjured up in the country'. They are intimately linked to geographical location. They, are less talkative than the good people. The accounts of the witch Isabel Gowdie are interesting as she says in her confession that it is the Devil that sharpens the Elf arrows and prepares their powers. She had seen this in her visits to Elf land. She also said that witches make these Elf arrows by forging coffin nails. The confessions of Isabel Gowdie are found in the third volume of Pitcairn's *Scottish Criminal Trials*. It seems from her account that each 'Covin,' or assembly of witches, had a maiden, and "without our maiden we could do no great thing."

Kirk says "They contain little or nothing of the 'psychical' all is mere folklore, Fairy tales, and charms derived from the old Catholic liturgy." This comment is yet another that would indicate that the 'old religion' indeed was derived from the Catholic faith and the use of the word 'coven' amongst present day revivalists is derived from the Roman Catholic convents. This assumption is further strengthened by noting that the 'Old Catholic liturgy' and 'Fairy beliefs' were quite often ascribed to the same practitioners.

Seers gifted to communicate with familiars and devils are called *Tabhaisver*. Kirk identifies these people with the Biblical witch of Endor whom King Saul consulted to communicate with the prophet Samuel. This suggests both necromancy and pyromancy.

They are reputed to 'have nothing of the Bible' and possess a vast number of charms and counter-charms and be related to werewolves and shape shifters. At its heart lies the deliberate use of the inhabitants of the kingdom of the dead. Kirk mentions that witches are using the souls of the condemned to do their bidding and he is suggesting that there is a difference when the spirits of the dead come voluntarily. When summoned like the *taibhshe,* meaning 'deaths messenger' they arrive in the shape of a dog.

Carlo Ginzburg's work, *Ecstasies, Deciphering the Witches Sabbath* looks at areas of Friuli, Italy. He segments the practitioners into two categories; similar to Kirk. In Ginzburg's account these opposing practitioners are called *benandanti* and *malandanti*. The *benandanti* secure good fortune and harmony for society. The *malandanti* do what they can to create disorder. Ginzburg reveals common ground with Kirk and also practices of the Craft, not only in Italy, but elsewhere on the continent. We shall look at

Ginzburg and the Witches' Sabbath in Germany and England in the next chapter.

Genii loci, djinns and the blood of nymphs

Stories and legends about these beings are found from Africa to Iceland. In the reign of Elizabeth the 1st, 'The Fairy Queen' they are found in the works of William Shakespeare. Various theories have been advanced to explain why Fairy encounters diminished over the last 500 years. The Ashanti in Upper West Africa have a legend of how these spirits rejected humans because of our deceptive wicked inclinations.

The idea of *genius* and *genii loci,* the Latin word for a tutelary spirit have become erased from our consciousness. This is a disturbing degeneration of spiritual values that in turn is reflected in the dislocated hunt for the magical or spiritual path. Little thought is offered to the spirit of the place i.e. the geographical location, or the *daimon* that is trying to guide you on the path of fate. Curiously the genii loci have recently found a place within modern architecture through the work of Bangs and Norberg-Schulz. It is as if the spirit of operative Masonry is calling the spirits of the land. We also have Feng Shui based upon the power born by the inhabitants of the land.

The Romans often depicted the genii loci in the form of a snake. The serpentine imagery is quite stunning and we see the same appear in the lore of Djinns, the fair denizens of the Arabic deserts, oases and gardens. Actually, if we look closer it can widen our perception and understanding of the ambivalent reputation of the Fairies.

Etymologically Djinn or jinni may be derived from 'genii' or 'genius'. Alternatively the word Djinn may originate from the Semitic root 'jnn',

THE GENII LOCI DEPICTED ON A ROMAN BASS RELIEF. CA. 65 C.E.

found in the word Jannah, 'Garden' or simply 'Garden of Eden'. The word describes an oasis or garden that is hidden or veiled and unseen by ordinary perception. It is the heart that gazes into paradise. These ideas are reflected in the notion of Elphame. Like the Fairies or the Scandinavian elves, the Djinns can be the malevolent aid of the sorcerer or good aids, akin to a daimon or guiding spirit.

The ambivalence is also found in the classes of Djinns, like the Ifrit and Marid. The latter is said to dwell at the castle and are masters of the weather. The Ifrit are vile and fiery Djinn, dwelling in desolated places assuming serpentine forms. Iblis is said to be the King of the Ifrits, intimately linked to another class of Djinns, Shaitans. These djinns are full of resentment and delight in intrigue, deceptions and consider every human enslaved as a victory. They can take a number of forms ranging from serpent and jackal to beautiful women.

Note the similarities between accounts of the daring consequences of dealing with Djabs in Haiti, a creolization of the French 'Diable'. Or the considerable care that must be taken by those in Scandinavia who sought the aid from the Black Elf. Clearly, Elphame, Hades or Hel(l) are intertwined worlds.

One of the vehicles for contacting the other side was the art of necromancy. In Isidore of Seville's *Etymologies*(Book VIII) he lists practices that are condemned as magical on the grounds of demonic illusion. These include any kind of divination (augurs, oracles and necromancy), remedies that use incantations, signs and amulets. Burchard of Worms add to the list: funeral walks and eating offerings to idols at tombs, springs, trees, stones, crossroads, honoring Jupiter, and dressing a stag at midwinter. Burchard's treatise is noteworthy since this is one of the common accusations used in the act of burning witches. Burchard speaks of many kinds of *superstitio* in the Greco-Roman world, the belief in satyrs and goblins, werewolves, forest nymphs and the Three Fates, basic tenants of the traditional Craft even today.

These ecstatic encounters with the other side went through a process of degeneration. Women and sexuality in particular were subject to condemnation. The worst acts of Devil-related practice were often seen in the vivid imagery of lewd or ugly women engaged in rituals of love and death. These women rode with demons at night or the Roman Diana or the Germanic Hulda/Holda. The rides to the Sabbath feast were common accusations in European Witch-craze of the late 15th and 16th

Centuries. In Hagiographies of this period one reads of saints seeing through the illusions of demons and repelling them, armed with the word of God and the Sign of the Cross.

The antidote to magic was Christian faith. The saints became the magicians of the new faith. The icons and statues of saints substituted idols of the pagan gods. Boniface, the missionary to the Saxons, converted existing practices into Christian ones, by giving new meaning to established cults. He told the cunning people to recite prayers over their charms and amulets and use the sign of the cross to bless objects. In such ways, the 'old faith' shed its skin and the legacy of the untamed ones was continued.

A ritual for feeding the Witches of the Land

Here, in the earth lies the blood and bones of our ancestors. We feed the earth, the womb and mouth of the world. Choose well if the Moon shall be of Blood or Milk. Under this Moon, veiled or exposed you will go to the might tree, be this Oak or Rose, Willow or whatever your heart tells. At its root you will fashion from fallen branches a cross with equal arms and tie it up with grass or vines. Place this at the northern side of the tree and speak unto the cross the following words:

> *Four roads meet and four roads part*
> *At the centre of All*
> *I have come to commune*
> *With the Silent Ones*
> *By this Cross I summon*
> *The legacy of my Blood*
> *This is the True Cross*
> *The Cross of the journeyman*

That knows his station and

Sojourn

Allow me to dwell again

In the arms of my kin

Great Gods, undead and eternal

Hear me as I awaken you from your

slumber and silence

You will trace the earth sign for protection and communication as the
lonesome wanderer taught us, what is known as the compass of the wise
and the helmet of Ygg, white as bone or bone-dust. Place the cross over
it and with wine and milk feed it and the ground at each point and its
centre and affirm that you are of pure determination and orientation:

Under the Star

I resurrect the Cross

I have journeyed to this point

Where all is still

I will discard all falsehood

And walk on within the

Pastures of the Golden Queendom

Under the star I stand

I am not fallen

Under the star I pray to thee

My fair daimon

Of my own True essence

My spirit guards

And alleys of the Night

Who all have brought me

To this Point

Under the Star

Where I raise

The True Cross

That trembles down

All falsity by its great powers

As One in the company

Of many I have raised

The True Cross under the Star

Now take up the cross and make a small hole in the earth and feed it a single drop of your own blood, taken from the longest finger on your left hand. Now moisten three black beans in your mouth and place them in the hole together with one silver coin. Place the cross over the hole and call the Mighty Dead:

Awaken from the slumber ye Mighty Dead

Of this Blessed Land!

Awaken and rise from the silent chambers at the heart of the earth

It is I........who have called thee

By blood and sign

By Heart and coal

By the Law that binds the True

By the garland of roses

And the Mystery of the Skull

By and through these sacraments

I summon thee to the banquette of One

Come to my aid fair and foul

Fairy host and the brides of Death

Skinleapers and undead ones

All you wise ones that once

Stepped on this earth

I summon you to once again step on this soil

So break out from the kernel of silence

Break out from within the earth

And see me as I draw the sign of the

Becoming One with the Ancient Blood

And see me as I feed the ground

To awaken you all to rise within

This Feast of One

And impart to me

The answers I am seeking

And give to me

The remedies I am needing

And come to my aid

In this hour of Need

By sacrament and the power of the Heart

By gifts and sincerity

By my Oath

I call thee

To witness the call of One of

Your own kin

Awaken!

Awaken!

Awaken!

Amen! Amen! Amen!

Rest now your head upon the cross and allow the spirit of the necropolis under the roots to take you, answer you, to guide and bless you. Then bring the cross to your lair and by night when you wish your blood to rush in your veins and administer to your needs, place it on a shrine level with your head together with a glass of blood red wine and water to the side of the cross decorated with bamboo leaves. By this necromantic act the dead shall speak and the blood turn against the grain for you so you may behold thy legacy and the wisdom or folly that is to come.

GENII LOCI - BY AUDREY MELO

4

Within the Mountain of Dame Venus

"...and she is called Lucifera,[15] *i.e. bringing light, bringing the years of the Sun to light; and she is called* Hesperus, *when she follows the Sun, and* Phosperus, *because she leads through all things though never so hard"*

- Cornelius Agrippa; Three Books of Occult Philosophy: 427

In the world of contemporary occultism ideas of traditional Craft are often shaped by a dualism. This perspective took hold in the western world with the propagation of Christianity. St. Paul in his Acts states that "The God of this World has blinded the minds of the unbelievers".

The ante Nicean (3rd Century) *Acts of the Disputations* with Manes asserts: "That man worships two deities, unoriginated, self-existent, eternal, opposed the one to the other. Of these he represents the one as good, and the other as evil, and assigns the name *of Light* to the former, and that of *Darkness* to the latter."[16]

We see here a metaphysics that insists on the existence of two equal but opposed substances. From a traditional perspective this view is untrue and here lies the root of the modern condition. Modernity insists on an order based on inclusion/exclusion or sameness/otherness. Modern man insists on categorizing the world in terms of good and evil.

Democracy, from the word 'demos', meaning 'commoner' or 'vulgar' where the common man insist on the value of his own voice. The modern political ideal reflect a traditional decay. Especially the insistence of man having the right to be whatever he wants and not what he ought. A monist model seeks layers of meaning that lead to unity. A dualist perspective insists on the importance of antagonism and rivalry. The separation between mind and body generates distance between man and the celestial domains. Thus was born the spirit of contemporary materialism in the West. This division between mind and matter affects the understanding of sexuality and the virtues of Venus.

Venus is today the Goddess of the *Ars Veneris*, of sexuality and beauty, usually understood from a very materialist perspective. We see a similar degeneration of Lucifer. In spite of the growing awareness of Lucifer being radically different from Satan, Lucifer continues to be merged with the image of Satan giving rise to a misanthropic and hateful being. It is rare today to see the traditional rendering of Lucifer as the 'bringer of light', who in his wise foresight cast his illuminating fire over the world. Little is said about his association with Apollo as a deity of the day and Dionysus as a deity of the night. And even less is said about his similarities with Vulcan or Adad of the Assyrians.

Adad was said to contain the light of all stars in the symbol of the Sun and was therefore identified with the Hebrew Schemesh, a deity who could be seen as masculine or feminine. The astrolabe of God if you will, as it unfolds in Sun, Moon and Venus; the two Great Lights of the Heavens and the Bringer of Light. This simple trinity is replicated in the notion of an astrological trine. The relationship of perfect love is signified by the segmentation of the zodiacal circle into 120 degrees. It replicates the completeness of the zodiac circle. Modern Luciferian witchcraft is actually a reconstruction of several mystical and folkloric elements. In the Orphic hymns to the Sun we see the symbols of Lucifer, such as Phoebus (beauty); and how he gives splendour and light to all things.

In Venus we see a rich imagery related to fortune and destiny. Agrippa refers to her as a mother whose tender affection saves her children from misery. But also that she humbles the high, strengthens the weak, makes noble the vile, rectifying and levelling all things. She is also referred to as the first parent and the power that by love and delight joins the sexes. She has a particularly bountiful disposition towards the mortals.

The Venusian theme as manifested in the crafts and arts of the countryside focused mainly on Venus as the Bringer of Light from the Moon. She rests in the gardens of both Sun and the Moon, night as much as day. The Moon or "Nightwalker" filters the various lights from the planets and stars to the Earth. Venus brings the multi-spectrum lights from the Moon to the Earth as a wide array of love, beauty and fortune.

In Northern Europe she was Frau Holt or Holda, who lives in the Venus Mountain. In Norway she is Huldra, a night-riding beauty upon a wild boar or pig. She brings eroticism, dreams and nightmares. In Henrik Ibsen's play *Peer Gynt* the protagonist is a dreamer and vagabond who experience a seductive encounter with this boar-riding beauty in the wild mountains. This dramatic event alters his life. The beautiful seductress manifests in the rays of the Moon, and brings Peer Gynt possibility and choice. She moves him, like the Holy Spirit moves the priesthood.

Venus as her day riding power manifests in Norse Freya, intimately linked to the Mercurial Odin. Freya with her seductive appetites and beauty is the power of the crossroad.

At times she is associated with Hel, an aspect of Holda. Ishtar's meeting with Ereshkigal is an initiatic drama playing itself out on the canvas of Venus.

The Witches Sabbath

The nocturnal convent of witches known as the Witches' Sabbath is marked by Venus, the Moon and the crossroad. In a specific aspect of the Moon the spirit goes to the crossroad at night to meet the Devil. As well as being the Queen of the Venus Mountain, we might see her as the power that animates. Testimonies of what went on at the Sabbath were largely accounts of obscenity and excess. The witches travelled by air in the night to meet their master and initiator. This Mystery is intimately linked to folklore all over the world, such as the Varcolac in Romania, the Vetalas in India and Carlo Ginzburg's night battles. Ginzburg is preoccupied with the areas of Trieste and Friuli, bordering the Slavic regions, where the legends and myths of night flight are many and detailed. This specific association between witches, lycanthropy and vampires will be further disclosed in the sixth chapter.

Emma Wilby in her study about the cunning folk in Northern Europe and in particular the British Isles comments that "the Sabbath was more commonly described as occurring in churches and churchyards, or out of doors."[17] Janet Hewitt in 1661 claimed she attended Sabbaths at a place called Muryknowes where the nocturnal gathering was celebrated with ale, bread and meat.

In the same year, Helen Guthrie claimed that she and nine other witches gathered in the churchyard of Forfar where they sung "the old ballads" and danced with the Devil, who she described as a "black iron hewed man". Elizabeth Styles in 1665 claimed that she had consumed wine, cakes and meat at these gatherings. The man in black brought all this bounty to the gathering whereupon they danced and made merry and when they left the gathering hailed each other with the words "merry meet, merry part". As some of you might be aware, this greeting was used by early Freemasons and is still used in quite a few lodges.

The term 'Witches' Sabbath' is of a fairly recent provenance and seems to have originated from Germany. The Papal Inquisition thought they had discovered a new heretical sect of Devil-Worshiping witches. Since they were a cult they possessed some secrets and naturally needed to convene. As Kittredge points out, the witches had always been subject to hatred and disrespect by the majority for failing to conform to rules and regulations, but also because they benefited from gifts of supernatural power. Even today, people who have problems conforming are subjected to accusations of various kinds.

The idea of an organized cult of Devil worshipping witches had no reality until in the 14th Century when it surfaced in the mind of the Inquisition. Kittredge suggests that this was a transference from the Cathari heresy to the cunning folk.

The trials reveal how in Germany the idea of an organized cult grew. In Britain the witches were tried as individuals for criminal acts. Until the 1540s these accusations were tried by civil courts. Trials concerning the Witches' Sabbath do not ever occur until the reign of James the first. The Inquisition was preoccupied with heresies within the confinements of the Church. Only on the continent, in Germany and France do we find these accusations. In England they confessed to having familiar spirits, such as dogs, toads and cats and to performing malefic magic. As late as the Chelmsford trial in 1589 there are no references to the Witches' Sabbath.

All these trials and confessions resulted in a tract written by the Reverend George Giffard, published in 1593 detailing witchcraft beliefs in Essex, but no single mention of feasts or sabbatical orgies. What we find is a reference to beliefs "in Germany and other countries", describing shape shifting into wolves that fly to a night banquet.

Reginald Scot spoke about this, but he was railing against beliefs on the continent, found in the *Malleus* and the writings of Bodin and Danaeus. In addition he was extremely skeptical of the idea of an organized cult of witches engaged in Devil worship. The first time the issue of the Sabbath surfaced was in Scotland in the 1591 confessions of Lady Newes. Even if the demonic pact was a reality, the Sabbath was not. The witch was considered to be a loner. She might have other companions, but they were hardly organized.

The first account of the Witches' Sabbath in any British trial is Lancashire witches of 1612. Anne Whittle confessed to having been admitted to the witches' circle by the witch Elizabeth Southerns. She said that after midnight the Devil came to Elizabeth's house and they went out to meet him. They partook of a meal and their familiars took the remnants. Elizabeth's daughter was also charged and told that at one point some twenty witches came to their home, two of them men, with the purpose of naming her familiar and to plot the murder of Thomas Lister. Elizabeth's daughter said after they had wined and dined the witches left in human form, but away from the house they took on the shape of horses, fowl and other animals. However, it was the conspiracy to murder Thomas Lister that most concerned the court and it was on these grounds that they were convicted.

This is the first of quite a few accounts in the 1600s referring to Sabbath like meetings including night-flight, shape-shifting and *malefica*. But as

Kittredge says: "There is not the slightest evidence that they were organized at all. Some of the accused were innocent, some were guilty in intent. Now and then, like other criminals, a few of them may have met to eat or to plot a murder. But 'covens' and Devil-priests and Satanic orgies are, for England, out of the question."[18]

Ginzburg details night-flight and shape-shifting amongst Italian and Slavic witches. His research demonstrates the following. The theme of the Witches' Sabbath crystallized in the middle of the 15th Century, in the paranoid compendium *Malleus Maleficarium* which set the standard for the witch and her beliefs. For instance the phenomena of skin-leaping became demonized as late as the 15th Century. Prior to this, those suffering from this affliction were considered to be innocent victims, often subject to a hereditary condition that affected their psyche or soul.

In the 5th Century BC Herodotus spoke about men who were periodically transformed into wolves. Likewise, in Africa, Asia and Scandinavia these bestial metamorphoses were believed to exist, whereby people turned into jaguars, wolves, dogs, leopards or the like. In 1555, Olaus Magnus, Bishop of Uppsala, Sweden described how werewolves in Prussia (Germany) broke into people's homes, drank their beer and slaughtered them. In this case a feast of stolen beer and human flesh. Considering this shift in perception Ginzburg says:

"During the same period the hostile image of the witch crystallized. This is not a mere coincidence. The Formicarus Nider *speaks of male witches who transform themselves into wolves; in the Valais trials, at the beginning of the 15th century, the defendants confessed that they had temporarily assumed the shape of wolves when attacking the cattle. From the very first evidence about the Sabbath, the connection between witches and werewolves therefore appears to be quite intimate."[19]*

The same motif is found in the 16th and 17th Century in the Italian countryside, more specifically Friuli, where the term *benandanti* was given to women who participated in the procession of the dead. It was also referring to others, many of them men, who declared that they were going out at night with fennel stalks to fight for the fertility of the crops against the *malandanti* armed with canes of sorghum. They further said that they took on the shape of mice, butterflies, hares or other animals to either journey to the procession of the dead or in their night fights. It is unclear in Ginzburg's account whether we are here encountering two different classes of witches or if these terms refer to the same witch but in his or her aggressive and hostile aspect. However, this ambivalence is in itself interesting and probably reflects the growing social tension concerning witches in the 15th Century. Without going too deeply into the details we can list the following repeating themes:

- *They took on a different shape at night, while their bodies were as dead in their bed*

- *They went out to fight for the fertility of the land*

- *The fight was against malevolent witches or the malevolent dead*

- *The* benandanti *was intimately linked with the Mysteries of death, even the night flight they describe as a state of lesser death.*

- *The presence of herbs, such as the tripartite conjunction of asphodel, which is reputed for its connection with the Underworld, fennel for exorcisms and rue for protection.*

- *The presence of a mark, either invisible or visible, in the case of the latter this was usually a birth-mark or an eerie mole.*

- *The reference to 'devils' as their lovers and deities of power.*

It is interesting that the same elements are still found amongst practitioners in many areas of Italy. The sabbatical encounters by oneiric means. The importance of deities, such as the Grigori or watchers, condemned as fallen and diabolic in theology since Augustine. What seems to be absent is the sexual and cannibalistic element. I know personally about traditions with roots in Italy that have a complex theology and rituals solidly founded in astrology and classical magic. Whilst others lack this rich philosophical foundation and function more on devotion to the saints and congress with familiars.

The motifs discussed by Ginzburg consists of the following elements:

1. Nocturnal flight to either an imaginable or physical location
2. The presence of a devilish creature with initiatory power
3. The guidance and presence of animal familiars
4. Sexual rituals and anti social behavior
5. Blasphemy and denial of faith with the infamous pact where one's soul is promised to Satan

These are the classical themes found in the *Malleus Maleficarum*. For instance, pacts and denial of faith originated with the passage in Isaiah 28: 15. Here we read: "Because ye have said, we have made a covenant with death and with hell are we in agreement." The verse refers to the deeds of wicked people and "the companions of the Lie". Diabolic pacts were not something new, already in 370 a legend surfaced concerning St. Basil, the Bishop of Caesarea, who was said to have retrieved from a devil a contract made by a lovelorn man to secure the heart and lust of a woman.

More famous were the legends of Theophilus who died around 538. This orthodox cleric was canonized and his feast-day is on February 4th. He was appointed archbishop for a large parish in Turkey but given his humble nature he declined the position. The one installed in his place was everything but humble and stripped Theophilus of his position as archdeacon. Filled with regret he contacted a wizard who summoned the Devil to make a compact. In return for the bishopric the Devil demanded in a contract written in blood, that he renounce the Holy Virgin and Christ. After some years Theophilus had second thoughts about the whole deal and prayed for forty days to the Holy Virgin for absolution. Theophilus woke up the following morning with the contract on his chest. He went to the bishop who burned the contract. As it went up in flames Theophilus drew his last breath but died absolved.

As mentioned earlier Gerbert, who became Pope Sylvester II, was also reputed to have sought the aid of the Devil to be Pope. The same was the case with Benedict IX. From 300 onwards the same accusations were made of bishops, priests and friars. What we see is that pacts were not uncommon in the Church. This speaks of a certain reverence for the 'Lord of the World' amongst the clergy. Kittredge[20] in his study of witchcraft in England recounts several examples where the clergy enter the crossroad of witchcraft. He also comments on how the 'Synagogue of Satan' surfaced in the 14th Century along with the Plague. This term indicates that the relationship between witchcraft and 'jewry' were basically perceived as being the same antisocial Pagan activity.

He mentions the *Canon Episcopi,* a document dating from 906 in the possession of the Abbot of Prüm in Germany. The document in its original form dates back to the Synod of Ancyra as early as 314. It discusses certain 'errors' of women. These 'errors' were the belief in demons and phantasms and: "that they ride upon beasts with Diana, Goddess of the Pagans, and a countless multitude of women, passing through many regions in the dead of night."[21] It also speaks about the 'Black Arts' the ability to change a man's heart from hate to love, night riding with familiar spirits (animals and beasts), what we today would call astral travel, nocturnal meetings, divination and superstitious ceremonies at springs, wells and stones as well as charms and rites used in order to create change. The Church was quite occupied with purging its Roman Catholic remains.

The Witches' Sabbath grew into a threatening reality. Walter Map, as quoted by Kittredge, tells a rather stunning tale from the 12th Century. The story tells of a knight whose three children had their throats slit. When the fourth child was expected he prepared with fasting and prayer. During this period a stranger arrived and asks for hospitality, the child is born and they take turns watching the newborn. The stranger sees a 'revered matron', hovering with malign intent over the child. Making his presence known to the spirit he asks who she is, she replies she is a demon. The stranger brands her on the face with a glowing iron. The next day he tells the knight to call upon the lady he had seen in the room and sure enough she has been branded on the face. The curious explanation is that the noble lady has angered the demons that had used her form at night to execute their murderous deeds. He performed an exorcism and the demonic spirits flew out from her and vanished.

The same theme is found in the *Legenda Aurea* as well as in the accounts of St. Germanus of Auxerre (378 – 448). St. Germanus is a canonized saint of both the Orthodox and Roman Catholic Church and is known of in the Isle of Man, Wales and Cornwall. Together with Bishop Lupus he baptized the native Britons and secured victory against Pict and Saxon armies. Wales and Cornwall are locations with long traditions of the Wise Art. In his hagiography we find an account of demons visiting houses for food. They are called *bona mulieris*, good women. They were seen in the shape of women living in the city.

The same phenomenon was understood to be a willing act of night flying committed by these women. Elizabeth Lambe in 1653 presents this demonic vampirism as a deliberate act on her behalf of doing damage to the child. These were called *striges*.

The origin of the *strige* is synonymous with the lamiae. They are described as cannibalistic and vampyristic bird women. Kittredge describes a mosaic from around 500AD where the *striges* are depicted as birds with women's heads, remarkably similar to Sirens. *Lamia* was said to be a mortal woman in whom Zeus took a romantic interest. The children she bore were slain by Hera. Lamia died of grief and slays other children as revenge.

A similar myth is also found related to 'Gylou', a female spirit reputed to feed upon babies. A rational mind would of course see all this as a testimony of high infant mortality, but the spiritual context is interesting. We see that it is usually a woman that flies at night with murderous intent. Later these phenomena grew into the belief that certain malefic witches sacrificed babies so they could use the fat and blood in their ointment to facilitate the sabbatic congress. These accusations resulted in some absurdities. We see a fusion of *Lamia* with *strige* to become the 'witch'. The Jews, or rather, 'Pagan Hebrews' had legends telling of a similar spirit. Lilitu, who also took the shape of birds and had a taste for children. The term, 'synagogue of Satan' might reflect the transposition of the *strige* identified with Lilith.

Witches, Toil and Trouble

What we are left with is the presence of familiar spirits, night flight, shape-shifting, charms, cures, curses, spells, divination, even pacts with spirits. In the Lancashire trial Elizabeth's daughter refer to these witches as members of her family. From this we can conclude that the

HANS BALDUNG GRIEN, THE WITCHES' SABBATH (1510)

developments such as in the 18th Century the horseman's word and other groups of traditional Craft developed as hereditary witchcraft. We might assume that some of these traditions initiated people outside the family as a way of securing the 'old faith' or simply because of common interests. This is partly the origin of what we today call Traditional Witchcraft.

Other groups probably organized themselves according to a Masonic model. What is important here is to note that any Craft lineage shares some basic features, in spite of a rich variation of elements and teaching. Some possess quite complex mystical teachings whilst others are quite simple and related to practical spell craft such as cord magic and wort cunning. What seems to be common is the importance of ancestry and the need for silence both related to the art as well as to spiritual points of power. Furthermore there are Christian elements and similarities with Roman paganism. It seems to me that what we today refer to as 'traditional Craft' is the result of harmonious interactions between cunning folk, hereditary witches and scholarly practitioners, such as Freemasons or other adepts.

Beliefs ascribed to the witches were basically focused around three areas, spirit communion, fortune telling and the power of the word. The Church in the Middle Age possessed the power, when extreme conditions required such action, to utter the 'curse of God'. Papal letters quite commonly carried with them an anathema on those who failed to heed the contents. Keith Thomas writes how: "four times a year the general sentence of ex-communication by bell, book and candle was pronounced against all thieves, murderers and enemies of the Church. Laymen could also avail themselves of this ecclesiastical power of malediction."[22] It was not uncommon that members of the Church contacted their vicar or priest to help them with maledictions on thieves and the like. One example is the theft of ecclesiastical artifacts from a church in Barcelona in 1628, whereupon the Bishop placed a curse on the land around the church with the consequence that the crops were totally destroyed.

For the Protestants this was all wrong, to be able to do wonders or make effective curses would indicate that the cleric was manipulating the power of God. It was a short road from this to accusations of diabolism.

Similarly some people were gifted with this same power, to curse or to bless. These people were often Catholics, whilst those found in Protestant countries retained a distinct Catholic flavour in their spell work. Fasting had its magical use, as in the 'Black Fast', used as a means for focusing one's intent, and inflicting illness and death on one's enemies. Likewise the use of wine, hosts, candles, bells, incense and many other items to bless or curse, people, animals or crops. Basically, if a person could bless, he could also curse and not all of the churchgoing people considered that the priest alone would possess magical power. This lead to theft of sacramental bread for protective usage. The Black Fast was forbidden by the Bishop of Durham in 1577, which indicates the practice was indeed alive and well – and considered effective.

Keith Thomas says: "The most common maleficent technique was the use of image-magic, by making a model in wax or clay of the proposed victim and then sticking pins or bristles in the part to be afflicted. That this kind of magic was extensively practiced there can be no doubt. It had originated in ancient times and was well known both to the Anglo-Saxons and in the Middle Ages."[23] Given the extent of malefic images, tablets and dolls we might assume that there was reason for the general fear of witches. In the Tudor period these props surfaced all the time.

Most of these practices were defined as 'natural magic'. In this first book of Agrippa's *Occulta Philosophia* we find these types of workings, such as sticking a pig's heart with pins and broken shards. In recent editions of the same work we find quotations from the 1722 *Secrets merveilleux de la magie naturel et cabalistique du Petit Albert*. The work is ascribed to friar Albertus Magus and fuses natural magic and Kabbalah.

Here we find the well-known hand of glory. The raw material for the hand of glory is the left or right hand of an executed criminal, the fouler the better. All blood is pressed out and it is placed in an earthenware pot for fifteen days. The pot is heated, either by sunlight or in a furnace in order to extract all the fat. This fat is collected and mixed with sesame seed oil (which would indicate an Arab origin) and virgin wax. The candle is then fixed on the top of the fisted hand, between the ring and middle finger or the candle is cut in five pieces and placed on the top of each finger. This preparation is done under the influences of Sirius. The prepared hand is used to evade discovery during a house intrusion. Its function is described in the Ingoldsby legends:

Now open lock to the Dead Man's knock
Fly bolt and bar and band
Nor move, nor swerve. Joint muscle or nerve
At the spell of the Dead Man's hand
Sleep all who sleep! Wake all who wake!
But be as the Dead for the Dead Man's sake

Here we see the differences between what we today call high and low magic. Low magic, is low because it concerns itself with the terrestrial and the affairs of the lower world. High magic is more mystical in nature and from the 15th Century onwards a leaning towards Kabbalah is evident, as in *The Key of Solomon* and several other grimoires attributed to the Jewish King Solomon.

The Renaissance astrologer and priest Marsilio Ficino points out, in his *Three Books on Life* published in 1489, the difference between demonic and spiritual magic. For Ficino the use of spiritual forces is in itself a risky step and might lead to demonic congress. This is in contrast of placing oneself under the spiritual rays of a force already present. The act of evoking carried dangers, while prayers and appeals were of a different order. As recent research, in particular Owen Davies, suggests, the wise or cunning folk, or 'witches', were constantly in this field of tension and thus represented an ambiguous presence in society. This is a hallmark of the witch, their allegiance with the liminal state. The witch was part man, part animal and part spirit. He or she could take animal shapes and fly at night, leaving the body still, as in death. This 'spiritual anatomy' defied the accepted rules of society, so naturally accusations of diabolism attached themselves to these practitioners. The night flight was intimately related to the gifts of Holda, the Dame of the Venus Mountain.

Walkers in the Roads of Night

Tales of witches going out in the night are many. We find them all over Europe, in Asia and Africa. The stories of night flight overlap with the legends of lycanthropy and vampirism to such extent that often it is not easy to see difference between the witch and her nocturnal allies and familiars. Baldung Griens paintings of witches conclaves and meetings and also Goya's all exhibit the same themes. These are of the night the wild wood where the natural civilized order has been turned upside down.

Goats speak, old hags fly, fiendish creatures attend the gatherings, ecstasy and Gnosis are revealed.

Linguistically we see how the Italian Stregoni or Streghoi refers both to the witch as well as a night flying vampire. The Stregoni can be *benefici*, but, the element of night flight persists. Similar ideas are found in the Romanian Strigele and Strigoii as the Latin Strix or Striga. The flight shows the importance of birds, crows, ravens and owls, who live by night and are in league with the Stregoni. It is from these avenues, the way of Hel or the 'Venus road' wherein harkens the Wild Hunt.

ᛉ This Mystery is preserved in what is called, 'the witches foot', that of a bird, the trident, the Tau and the Rune Algiz. If we look at Algiz in relation to Freya, the Vanir who taught Odin *seidr*, or witchcraft, an important feature is revealed. This is the intimate relation between night flight, ecstasy and the powers Venus holds by virtue of her essence. *Seidr* assumes the ability of night flight to gain power. The few accounts we have from Snorre's *Edda* suggest that *seidr* is possible partly by the aid of the familiar and the ability to entering ecstatic trance-flight.

When Odin hung from the tree to gain insight into the Mysteries of the Runes he was seeking secrets hidden within the mountain of Venus. This act is a repetitions of the motif of Shemyaza, who as a penalty for his disobedience was hung upside down in the constellation of Orion. The hunters girdle, has three stars representing the triple powers of Venus. The central star, *alnilam*, means 'string of pearls' and bestows public honour. The lowest star, *alnitak*, gives grain and nuts and was by Al Biruni called 'the delight of Venus'. The third star, *mintaka*, is traditionally a bringer of good fortune. Oral lore from Spain tells how Orion stoops

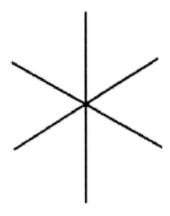

THE WITCHES' FOOT, THE DEVIL'S TRIDENT.   ALGIS

towards his Queen, Cassiopeia. The same constellation Spencer made the throne of the 'Fairy Queen' in his play.

The Rite of Taking flight

The realm of the Nightshade

The mystery of night travelling is disclosed in the silent world of the 'herbs of solace' or 'flying ointment'. Iohannes Weyer, a student of Cornelius Agrippa, gives the following formulae: Sium (cowbane), acorum vulgare (sweet flag), pentaphyllon (cinquefoil) uespertilitoris sanguis (bat's blood), solanum somniferum (deadly nightshade) and oleum or oil.

Another traditional ointment uses root of liquorish, root of Mandrake, flowers and leaves of Datura Metel, Belladonna, Anis and oil. I would advise extreme caution with this recipe including variants utilizing aconite (monkshood).

Monkshood is a frequent ingredient in flying ointments, but can be a poison capable of paralyzing the lungs, so its use is not advocated. Belladonna is its antidote. This explains why most ointments using Monkshood also used Belladonna. To test your own sensitivity, gently cut(scratch) your own Venus-mountain (the one on the thumb) and place a piece of the root on the wound. Remove it after ten to fifteen minutes. Stay calm and receptive for one hour and see if this encounter generates any effect.

For spirit flight to the Master's Sabbath I would recommend the following philtre; take one teaspoon of Mandrake root, three leaves of Datura Stramonium or Metel and one flower of the same plant, a tablespoon of Belladonna berries (ripe), a tablespoon of liquorish root and a tablespoon of Hyssop. Place this in cognac sufficient for it to cover the herbs for a week and mix this with 1,5 litres of red wine. Let this rest for 24 hours and it is ready. Show caution, even with recipes likes this, whose intent is to counteract the deadly toxins.

Cut a piece of rosewood, blackthorn, fig or hazel into a wand in the shape of the witch's foot. Do this when the Moon is growing and in Taurus, Cancer or Libra, alternatively in a good aspect with Mercury. You can also do this on a Wednesday (Mercury's Day) in his first hour of the night. Leave an offering of ground coffee, milk, wine, honey and three coins in gratitude to the spirit of the tree.

> *in Agrippa's 2ⁿᵈ Book he says concerning the Moon in her exaltation: "From the operations of the Moon, they made an Image for travellers against weariness, at the hour of the Moon, the Moon ascending in its exaltation; the figure of which was a man leaning on a staffe, having a bird on his head, and a flourishing tree before him;"*

Take the staff, red wine and milk to a river in the hour when Venus is rising. Pray to the Fairies and declare this your wand is the ladder to the Sabbath. Prick yourself and anoint the top and bottom of the staff with your blood.

The next day, when Venus rises in the sky take a cord of leather the height of your body. Tie nine knots on the cord, one knot for each of the three fates and their threefold placement in time and space. Tie the cord around your staff.

On the third night bring the staff and a knife to the same place. Carve in the lower end of the ladder the Rune Hagal and while carving chant the words of otherness: Hel -Hagal- Hela. Carve the Witch's Foot on the top, and chant, in the language of the birds: Algiz—Algiza-Holda-Algiz. In the centre you will carve Laug and chant with the voice of fertile water: Laguz-Freya-Laugar.

Anoint the staff with oil and breath. Let it rest in a dark cloth in a dark place until the Full Moon. Avoid exposing it to the Sun.

On the appointed night, when Venus rises, take your staff and your Vinum or Unguent Sabbati and position yourself to the north and wait until the Moon rises. Make a petition to the Moon to take you on her wings to the Hidden Convent where you will anoint yourself.

Take the ladder and plant it in the ground repeatedly shouting:

Sator, Falcifer, the witches of the land
The Moon is full and fertile and I bid ye mighty dead to rise
From grave and alcove, from pound and woodhouse
Rise from your slumber and come to the ladder's steps

Then feed the wine and almonds to the earth. Place your left hand to the ladder and see in your mind's eye the skull faced legions rise from the ground.

Then say:

Of masters of the skull and wine, blade and cross
By your blood I call upon he who rideth out in the wild hunt
Hooded master of grove and pyre
Dark one at the door and crossroads
I beseech you to open the witch way to the sabbath
By the Fates so fair, and the Sisters Wyrd

Throw the silver thread across ladder and mount

Ninefold Mother, Hel, Herodias, Holda

Queen of Elphame, Queen of Venus' mount

Take me to the Hidden Convent!

Recite the journey Runes and focus on the Witch's Foot and ascend through the well of thorns to the sacred place behind the Moon. Let the witches of the land, Faunus himself or your familiar take you through the ladder and into the Sabbath circle.

To return again grip the ladder and shout:
Sator Rentum Tormentum.
In Nome Patri,
Filii et Spiritus Sancti,
by the skull of wisdom
and in the Master's name!

Upon return leave an offering of fig, apple and water to the *genii loci* and fair folk of that particular place.

By using the same spot for the sabbatic flight you will generate a portal and with greater and greater ease you will be able to traverse between the kingdoms.

NOCTURNA BY AUDREY MELO

5 The Vinculum of Eros

"Kabbalah teaches that there is a secret unity of all Being hidden within the multiplicity and diversity of life as we experience it. God and universe are related not primarily as Creator and creature, which sounds as though they are separate from one another, but as deep structure and surface. God lies within or behind the façade of all that is... We, in fact, discover the Oneness of Being by staying right here, paying as close attention as we can to the present in which we live." - Arthur Green; *EHYEH: A Kabbalah for Tomorrow*

Contemporary books of spellcraft, be it for harm or healing, rarely speak about the nature of *vinculum* or natural bonds. A spell's effectiveness is both enabled and limited by the inherent unity of all things and the internal sympathy found therein. Magistrates and magicians in the Renaissance and post-Renaissance, like Agrippa and the anonymous authors of the grimoires, mention the 'great vinculum'. The great vinculum is the secret behind all effective theurgy and magic. This *vinculum* or bond comes into action when the virtues of things natural are in harmony with their celestial mirror.

Agrippa relates this bond to the interaction between Venus and Cupid/ Eros as told by Virgil. In the 1st book of the *Aeneid* we learn how Cupid, on request from his mother Venus, "breaths secret fire of love's poison" as he exchanges a kiss with Queen Dido. Cupid is the power of attraction revealed in the fire of love. The fire of love is what sustains and upholds creation by encouraging change and transformation. When we see Cupid from this angle it is easy to understand both how the 'great vinculum' was revered for its tremendous power. It also sheds light on why magic and witchcraft was the focus of such great fear among the clergy. Cupid

DAMA VENUS - BY AUDREY MELO

worked through lighting the fire of man's passions, often overpoweringly so. Accordingly there are good reasons for treating this power with care and awe – even avoid it altogether. At its most sublime, Eros was the divine amalgam of transformation, in its most material it was pure lust and passion.

Eros, love, the erotic, the sensual and all forms of passion are fiery. Fire can give heat and life; fire can make barren and desolate. Jung saw this as the power of bonding, a feminine potency contrasting the male 'logos'. Plato saw Eros as the pulse of attraction towards completeness. In Eros is that great power that moves our daemon to the possibility of completeness. When we say we love another person it is because Eros has motivated us to see in the image of the beloved our own possibility for perfection.

The 12th Century, motivated by an order of poets, *Fedeli d' Amore* ('The Faithful of Love') saw the rise of troubadours and the concept of courtly love; an enactment of the lovelorn tension between the lover and beloved. 'The Faithful of Love' applied a form of noble and erotic spirituality with the aims of spiritual restoration for man and society. This ideal came to influence a great tradition of 'saints of Love', especially the Arabic Mystery poets of love, most famously Rumi. From the 13th Century the heritage from Dante contributed to a revitalization of the Cult of Mary and also the Neo Platonic revival of Kabbalah.

Love was so essential, because it was by finding one's centre in this field of transformation that restoration was made possible. It is common amongst Sufi initiates to see love as the divine place where contrasts and antinomies are reconciled. This observation speaks volumes for the tremendous potency found within Eros as the *vinculum* or bonding agent of effective magic. Matysendranath, the creator of the yogini-kaula, who saw in woman the presence of God, expressed similar ideas. By venerating the divine presence a restoration was set in motion.

The idea of finding one's centre in the field of passionate tension is vital. It is this dynamic that makes spellcraft work. It is this that we call the *vinculum of Eros* the secret mechanism of sorcery. We shall turn to Giordano Bruno to expand on the mechanism, but first we need to present the traditional worldview of Bruno's time.

Via Sacra and Mundus Archetypus

A world view shows one's place in the vastness of all. The late Rabbi Aryeh Kaplan suggested one start with simple acts of meditation and contemplation, known as *hitbonenuth*. Focus on a leaf, flower or an idea and from this allow the mind to be filled as a mirror for self-reflection. By seeing oneself reflected in the leaf you will see the divine within. This enables communication with the divine - with the source.

There is indeed a sacred centre, a common origin from where seeps forth the pathways of mystery. This is the world of *Nous*, the Divine Mind or *Mundus Archetypus*. This realm is quite different from psychoanalytic thought where archetypes are reduced to subjective structures below the world of divine platonic forms. Modern psychology and in particular psychoanalysis operate by looking within and downwards. Any connection to origin is severed and man becomes the product of whatever beliefs he imports from a dysfunctional world.

Modern man is 'searching for himself' by turning his eyes inwards. He does not see his happy destiny and prosperity, but a network of tangled choices that leads to nowhere. When a Magus or sorcerer, witch or whatever tries to work wonders in the world, nothing happens. The bonds of Eros are solely concerned with engaging the transcendent vertical spiritual dimension, the domain of the supra-human. The Magus is, as Cornelius Agrippa says *"...who doth...transcend the progress of the angels and comes to the very Archetype itself of which being then made a cooperator may do all things..."*

A term like archetype has become totally garbled and deformed. As Nigel Jackson comments: "Plotinus says that Kronos was Lord of the Golden Age because his name means Koros Nous, the *'Abundance of Divine Mind'* denoting the infinitude of the Archetypal Ideas within the Noetic World."[24] Modern man is like a spiritual beggar, their maps and compasses lost. Instead of the map, they create an approximation of the world and follow a broken intuition to an illusory north.

From the divine mind a golden chain is stretched and this was a common understanding of the world's interconnectedness in the Renaissance.

The Golden Chain of Being

The Chain of Being was one of the three ways the Elizabethans understood the universal order. The others were dance and society as a series of hierarchical orders. This idea was intimately connected with virtues as the riches of God's abundance stretching from the foot of his throne to the meanest of inanimate objects. Nothing in creation was seen as useless, everything had its place in a hierarchy, as links in the golden chain. This hierarchy assumed that all things had something above it and something below it. The idea of perceiving creation as a golden chain of divine virtue came from Plato's *Timaeus*. It spread through schools of Neo-Platonic thought during the Middle Ages until the 18th Century. The Chain of Being envisioned at least two ways of ascent into the divine embrace. As Tillyard says: "The Chain of Being is a means of spiritual ascent: but only in an ideal interpretation. God has a ceremonial as well as a natural law". This suggests the importance of Jupiter as the fountainhead for the Chain, providing a way to enlightenment through religious and ceremonial works. The hierarchy of the chain is said to the following:

1. The inanimate class of mere existence, -the elements, liquids and metals.

2. Life and Existence - the vegetative classes.

3. Life and feelings or the sensitive class where there are three grades being separated between living and sensitive beings having touch but not hearing, memory or movement, like shellfish and parasites. Then there are those who have touch, memory but no hearing, like ants and finally those animals that have all these faculties like horses and dogs.

4. These three previous classes lead to men who have all these faculties as well as understanding.

5. There is also a class that is spiritual and rational: angels that are linked to man by understanding but different from man by their lack of worldly attachment.

This orderly chain creates a dynamic where everything finds its place and function in creation and the world is harmonious and beautiful.

The stars and Lady Fortuna, ('pars fortuna') were equally important. The divine order is conceived of as a golden chain of virtue leading from the divine throne to all things in creation bringing providence, fortune and human character. Fortune was symbolized as a wheel presided over by Lady Fortuna. The planets were seen as the agents of communication between eternity and creation. Fortune could be both good and bad, thus replicating the cosmic qualities in one's life. The stars were considered malign and astrology was used in order to diminish their hostile influence.

These sentiments arose from the observation of man's material nature, thus the celestial ray was a burden. It created ambiguity as man realized a twain desire, upwards and downwards. The downward desire went towards individualization, with all its limitations. The upward desire reached towards the un-manifest in the celestial halls. It is this dual pull that is interpreted as dualism, a testing ground for the believer as much as for the unbeliever.

One could consider this as fatalism or with for instance Raleigh, as quoted by Tillyard, see one's condition as the "power of education in reinforcing or mitigating the effects of the stars."

This would be related to an ascent to the divine throne of God and thus the greatest malefic would be lack of understanding. As Tillyard says: "the Elizabethan believed in the pervasive operation of an external fate in the world. The twelve signs of the zodiac had their own active properties. The planets were busy the whole time; and their fluctuating conjunction produced a seemingly chaotic succession of conditions, theoretically predictable but in practice almost wholly beyond the wit of man."[25] This leads to the conclusion that man is in charge of his own destiny or Fortune since suffering is a lack of understanding of his connectedness with cosmos. This Basque word for 'witch', *sorginak*, literally means 'the one who makes his own fate'.

Agrippa in his Book I of *De Occulta Philosophia* presents a lengthy discourse on the nature and combination of elements. The elements were considered as parts in a perfect whole, not divided but rather segmented into a variety of aspects. The elements had a different meaning for the Elizabethan mind than in our modern age. They were thought of in terms of their effects, air and fire having an upward motion; while earth and water downward. Further the elements were "founded upon the notions of hot and cold, dry and moist. Earth as an element was the name for the cold and dry qualities of matter". Earth was considered to be the heaviest and lowest element due to its cold dry nature associated with the dregs in the center of the world. Outside the earth are the waters, which are cold and moist.

Outside the waters is the hot and moist Air. Air was considered nobler than water. Then finally fire, which was hot and dry ,the noblest of elements associated with divinity. Fire, due to its invisibility and power was equated with the Divine. Devils and demons were often ascribed to the same elements. Djinns for instance were made from smokeless fire, storms or hot winds. Whether the element is bad or good depends on subtle differences. Benefic angels were seen in the heat associated with fire. It was the 'invisible fire'. In the same manner, the still fresh or soothing wind heralded good angels and spirits. Love played itself out in these contrasts. The elements were in constant transmutation, shifting their weight and balance, thus Ovid says:

"Nor can these elements stand at a stay/ But by exchanging alter every day"

The harmonious interaction of all things was mirrored in the playfulness of the elements, man's mutability and natural state.

The Elizabethan worldview, like any raditional worldview, was geocentric. The center of the human affairs and the place of Fortune was the material world. We have a double nature partaking both in the kingdom of angels as well as of beasts; a bridge between the celestial and telluric, partaking in all three worlds (Ideas, Celestial and Material).

In Iamblichus *Life of Pythagoras* we read that "Man is called a little world not because he is composed of the four elements but because he possesses all the faculties of the universe…Being an amalgam of many and varied elements, we find our life difficult to order."[26] Our different faculties pull us in different directions. Man's body partakes of all elements by the quality of the humors.

The cold and dry elements cause melancholy. The cold and moist elements corresponded to Phlegm. The hot and moist elements of the air corresponded to the blood. The hot and dry element is the Bile. These temperaments must be balanced. This was the natural order replicated in man, 'the little world' .

Our anatomy corresponding with the universe; its order but our double nature is as beast and angel. Thus the idea of a battle between reason or passion. There was only one solution to this, self-knowledge. The knowledge of self was considered 'the gateway to all virtue', the great enemy was within and without seeking to understand we could never be victorious and realize the little world, the mirror of the cosmos.

Spells of binding and the sorcerous road

The effective mage or sorcerer will ultimately be a good person, free from moral judgement. He or she is a person whose understanding of the divine order reflects a respect for creation and who possess a deep understanding of its inherent unity. The secret of creation is found in love, the erotic field of unity, its cornerstone.

The art of binding is founded in the theory of creation that sees the sympathy between things. The most direct example of binding is knot magic, a practice found in every corner of the world. Bruno in his *De vinculum in generis*[27] presents the clearest account. He starts by drawing attention to the various bonding agents. He lists them as God, demons, souls, animals, nature, chance, luck and fate. It is through these agents the power is found. In order for a binding to be effective we need to understand the relationships. If we take love between two people we can dissect matters, subtle and crude. The bonding is physical and intellectual attraction, various pledges, emotional bonds, finances, children, possessions, stars: the body as well as the psyche. To use the language of modern psychology, an effective bonding is to find the stimulus that reinforces your partner's desire to stay with you. These can be varied and depend on the partner's preferences. Bonds can be forged by lust, smell, gifts, threats – the list is endless, just like the golden chain of being itself. Things move with more ease towards that which they are inclined.

As Bruno comments: "An artisan binds with his art, for art is the excellence of the artisan". This is the premise for the witches' art. A binding must be done with sympathy, either for a connection already there or a link that can be forged by artificial means. Eros is the strongest and most radical of all bonds.

Bonding depends on the appetite, the available powers. There are agents that binds by their own power, what in Vodou is referred to as *pwen* or point. Several natural items are considered *pwens*, such as a hagstone or a tree struck by lightning (other *pwens* can be created). As Bruno summarizes elegantly in *De Vinculum* (Chapter 1 vs 29):

> *"A bonding agent does not unite a soul to himself unless he has captured it; it is not captured unless it has been bound; he does not bind it unless he has joined himself to it; he is not joined to it unless he has approached it; he has not approached it unless he has moved; he does not move unless he is attracted; he is not attracted until after he has been inclined towards or turned away; he*

is not inclined towards unless he desires or wants; he does not desire unless he knows; he does not know unless the object contained in a species or an image is presented to the eyes or the ears or to the gaze of an internal sense. Bonds are brought to completion by knowledge in general, and they are woven together by feelings in general.[28]

The senses, nature and the imagination are the faculties utilized in order to effect this art. The observant one sees that relationships both mundane and celestial are ruled by the same factors. A hungry man will be bound to eat any kind of food placed in front of him. A woman who considers you ugly and repulsive will not naturally be inclined to be bound to you. Simple spells such as boiling sugar and water wherein the name of the person you seek to calm is placed, will almost always accomplish its aim because humanity is inclined to be sweetened. Spells to harm people, to cause accidents, misfortune and death are far more difficult to accomplish, because they do not follow the natural flow of love and Eros.

The basic four factors involved in bonds are mind, soul, nature and matter. Mind is stable; soul is moveable; nature partly stable and partly moveable; matter moveable and stable. It is crucial to make cunning use of these faculties. For instance a person that comes across as *eagle-like* will most likely be bound by the things that will bind an eagle. A woman that manifests qualities of Venus will most likely be bound by the very same agents.

The stars have specific dominion over geographical locations as they have over men, beasts and plants. The more we know about the target the more we can forge Cupid's bond and the more we can wreck malediction or benediction on the person.

Necromantic practices, curses and the manufacturing of a poppet in the image of the person follows the same basic thinking. Here it is essential to have 'volts', i.e. nails, bones, hairs, fluids etc of the person as this will infuse the image with the essence. To take the footprint of someone, the name itself inscribed on metal, virgin paper or tablets of wax or clay can also create the desire *vinculum*. These avenues are related to the *Via imaginibus* or 'way of imagination' and the utility of the spells depends on the artist's capacity and mastery.

Let us look at some different forms of bonds, namely:

Location and temperament according to planet and sign

The popular Hermetic axiom 'As above, so below' is crucial for effective bonding. Agrippa and Thomas Aquinas realized that everything, from buildings to garments receive a certain quality from the stars. Agrippa comments (II: 35): "for the beams of the celestial bodies being animated, living, sensual, and bringing along with them admirable gifts, and a most violent power, do, even in a moment, and at the first touch, imprint wonderful powers in the images".

In plain words, all forms of action and creation are moved and mediated by celestial powers. This can cause good and bad consequences, luck and misfortune.

The word 'magic' is probably derived from the Latin word *imagio*, meaning image, probably a reference to the Persian magi's preoccupation with *telesma*, or talismans. The word *imagio* also refers to the power of creating heavenly images. Today the imagination has connotations of fantasy, the illusory and the unreal. The planet doctors in classical times made no such distinction. The further a plant was from its influence the greater the differences in the display of its virtue. The classical form of bonding is the talisman. Natural items, such as plants, metals, stones and animals were considered extremely helpful for capturing the celestial rays especially when there existed a bond between natural items and planets.

For instance Agrippa says of the images of Venus the following:

"From the operations of Venus they made an image, which was available for favour and benevolence at the very hour it ascended into Pisces, the form of which was the image of a woman with the head of a bird, and feet of an eagle, holding a dart in her hand. They made another image of Venus to get the love of women, in the lapis lazuli, at the hour of Venus, Venus ascending in Taurus, the figure of which, a naked maid with her hair spread abroad, having a looking glass in her hand, and a chain tied about her neck, and nigh her a handsome young man holding her with his left hand by the chain, but with his right hand making up her hair, and they both look lovingly on one another, and about them is a little winged boy holding a sword or a dart. They made another image of Venus, the first face of Taurus or Libra or Pisces, ascending with Venus, the figure of which was a little maid with her hair spread abroad, clothed in long and white garments, holding a laurel, apple, or flowers in her right hand, in her left a comb. It's reported to make men pleasant, jocund, strong, cheerful, and to give beauty."

Volts (nails, bones, hair etc)

Agrippa's First Book of *De Occulta Philosophia* treats in detail this field of natural magic. Many spells tell how to manufacture oils and unguents from various animal parts during the culination of Sirius, the Dog Star in the month of July. Sirius influences thieves, for good or ill. Remedies for protection against theft as well as making the thief's business more prosperous were done under this star.

Volts, meaning hair, nails, skin, body fluids represent a part of the greater unit and thus gives access to the totality. Likewise, a tree struck by lightning will take on the power of lightning and can be used for protection and destruction.

Witch bottles for protection usually contained sharp objects and the owner's urine. Urine is a magnificent anti witchcraft remedy, a substance like blood, but with an amazing effect on filthy influences.

Pliny tells how a menstruating woman walking naked amidst the corn fields in the hour before sunrise will repel all insects and plagues. If done at midday she will make the corn wither. Likewise Pliny recalls the fumigation made by animal parts: burning the lungs of a donkey repels flies. The knowledge of herbs, perfumes and fumigations were so great amongst the witches before the 15th Century, it was common to refer to them as 'venefica' or poisoners. The court of King James I was riddled with sorcerous scandals.

This image of the witch as poisoner and herbalist is also seen in the various powders of the mischievous Haitian Bokor, which can turn you into a mindless zombie. We have here two examples, the poppet and the mojo bag, also known as *patua* or charm bag, all making use of *volts*. These two items, the mojo bag and the poppet has become deeply associated with Vodou, due to the reputation of New Orleans witch doctors Dr. John and Marie Laveau. These techniques have been with us for a long time. The mojo bag is a talisman and the poppet uses the image of a person to harm or cure. British cunning man Cecil Williamson used this magic. Variations of the mojo bag are found amongst many contemporary Craft groups, especially those with an interest in plants magick.

A Poppet spell for healing

For this spell obtain *volts* from the person in need of healing and fashion a doll in their likeness. You can make the doll from clay, solid paraffin wax or some other substance. Take marigold, rue, rosemary, thyme and basil, dry it and mix with the doll. Make a "heart" from pure beeswax and place it on a bed of roses where you have written the name of the afflicted one on seven of the petals. Pray over and over by the heart of Jesus that the person gets well. Do this by the light of a single white candle and in the presence of pure water.

Make a cavity in the doll and place the heart inside. Make a brush from fresh coriander, rue and basil. Gently whip the doll with the water. Then take an egg and pass it over the doll on all four sides and throw it out to the south of the house. Take more water and clean the doll with the brush.

Then take white linen and the petals of seven roses and place upon it the doll and the brush on top.

Place the water and candle there and say:

> *All sickness Good St Peter whipped away*
> *All infirmities will now go to Hell*
> *The third time belongs to Good St Peter*
> *As the whip withers and dries,*
> *So will your sickness wither and disappear.*

A poppet spell for harm

Make a bread figure from flour, salt, peppers and vinegar, place the *volts* in the mixture. To curse the person, build up a blind anger while making and forming the doll. Put it in the oven and watch it turn black. Curse thy enemy constantly and when the doll is black, take it out and burn yourself a little and then throw the doll into a filthy place with the words:

Like a burned pig turn back to the filth from whence you came! (name the person)

Do this three times, turn your back, spit three times over the left shoulder and walk home without looking back.

A mojo bag for warding off malefica

Take the following ingredients:

Coffee beans, sea salt, rue, seven thorns from a red rose, an iron cross, tobacco, roots of fern and of spinach. On the Day of Mars in his hour, call upon the Lord of Spirit, War and Protection by his signs and tokens. Light three red candles and offer tobacco, Campari and red wine.

Mix the ingredients together in a red cloth and tie it with a black cord twinned three times around the packet. Take three sips of the Campari and spray it on the pack. Fumigate the bag with tobacco and leave it between the three candles until the next day.

The use of an external spiritual agent

Spells and magic happens when the witch is connected to the active spirit in question. The witch must bond with the world of matter and the spirit in the 'land' where they meet. The virtue of a plant or a mineral must be understood in light of the celestial body or denizen that presides over it. This can be by intuition or knowledge, but better both combined. The witch, or the one who is working the Craft, needs sensitivity and awareness of Nature. In many cases Nature teaches what is needed to make a spell effective. All magical acts use a spiritual agent, because all things are ensouled. Creation is living and has a pulse. The pulse of the Earth beats to the rhythm of the celestial abodes.

All have a *daimon* who speaks in the language of dreams, intuition and visions. This *daimon* has a very soft voice and can be drowned in the noise of modern living and material demands. The *daimon* is our spiritual double, our familiar given at birth. It is of air and heat, it draw us towards our fortune and destiny. Even a materialist man falls under the rulership of a spiritual virtue, like every other object in creation. Since we are spiritually animated we have access to understanding of spirits. Man as microcosm can manifest all things. Ideas of *agathodaimon* (good *daimon*) and *kakodaimon* (bad *daimon*) ultimately reflect on the character of the witch. It is here we find the meaning of negative and positive witchcraft.

The Art of Fascinatio

It is opportune at this point to return to the subject of *fascinatio*. This concept has largely been translated as 'the evil eye', the power of envy or jealousy projected upon people and livestock. This was the work of the eyes. The eyes, like water and mirrors, are suitable portals for spirits. In West Africa, the power of fascination, to control or to alter events by simple looks, words or actions is considered to be the hallmark of the witch. The other part is the oral spell, the charm, the act of attracting, or being attractive. Again we see the net of Cupid.

Apuleius in *The Golden Ass* described the effects of bewitchment as the eyes of the witch sliding down his own eyes and stirring his heart and marrow. Agrippa, in a similar vein, sees rays that the witch can project from her eyes but rooted in the heart.

Various collyriums (eye drops) were in Agrippa's time used by witches to enhance the projection of Eros or desire. The witch could use civet of cats or eyes of wolves turned into collyrium to induce fear or vaginal secretion to induce lust and attraction. This innate power was demonized and considered malefic, as one saw only the damage in 'casting the evil eye' or provoking lust. The study of optics by Albertus Magus and Francis Bacon was probably motivated by this fact that some people were naturally capable of allowing their heart to flow out from their eyes and influence their surroundings. The modern invention of the camera, was inspired by our ancestors interest in the art of fascination.

Actually, most people are capable of fascination. Breath and pulse together project one out from the eyes. When pulse and breath are harmonized with another person, the eye of the witch can truly walk down the bloodied shafts of one's soul and pull at his or her heart and nerves. This power is natural. Basically fascination is a highly condensed and well directed vapor from the realm of Eros. The heart of the witch beats as one and the eyes cause domination and control, evoking lust within the target.

The idea of malefica

Malefica is a complicated term. When a tumor is said to be malignant it denotes a parasitic growth. A person is referred to as malicious when they demonstrate anti-social character traits. From the Middle Ages up to the 18th Century, *Maleficarum* was used to denote individuals understood to be 'witches' hostile towards established society. Any person suspected of harbouring ill intentions, risked being labeled a 'witch'.

In astrology we understand Saturn and Mars to be the greater and lesser malefics. Likewise when planets are in square or opposition. Hostile relationships are those concerning dispute, feud, war, quarrels, misunderstanding, separation and litigation. Traditionally these are issues related to the 1st and 7th house in the astrological chart – the same houses for marriage and harmonious relations. So, very simply, *malefica* speaks of an antagonism in a relationship. This can be opposing a common consensus. In the Middle Ages, disagreement with the social norms could be sufficient to be accused of *malefica*.

Let us close this chapter on Love with the antagonistic workings in her domain, the curse. The curse was, and is, a consequence of oath breaking. The word is given and broken.

Lylet's Curse Cord

Mark yourself with *oil of destruction* on the forehead, palm of hands, heart and genital area. For each point say the following:

Lamassu – Izorpo – Lamassu – Ik – Thiltho

Lilithu – Lilithu – Lilithu

Odam – Odam – Odam

Take the cord and make nine knots with the name of the offender placed inside the knot. With perfect focus see your desire in your mind's eye and tie up the enemy.

The first knot I tie to bind your will	*Lil – Odam Ha!*
The second knot I tie to bind your heart	*Lil – Odam Ha!*
The third knot will bind your mind	*Lil – Odam Ha!*
With the fourth you are mine	*Lil – Odam Ha!*
With the fifth I drive you away	*Lil – Odam Ha!*
With the sixth I tie you down	*Lil – Odam Ha!*

With the seventh I take your sight   *Lil – Odam Ha!*

With the eight I take your voice   *Lil – Odam Ha!*

And may the ninth render you harmless! Lil – Odam Ha!

This I pray as She is my witness:

Here utilize either Thanatos or Eros to make the final charge, reciting in a repetitive fashion holding the cord in your hands in front of your mouth, so it takes your breath:

Lilith, Naamah Agrat bat Mahlat

Put the cord in a jar or bottle full of spikes and vinegar. Spikes can also be tied in the cord together with the name of the enemy.

State your will three times and recite:

Abito – Abyzu – Amizu – Avitu – Lamassu – Zahriel – Zefonith

Partashah – Satrina – Bituah – Lilith – Odam

May my will be done

May the evil be gone!

This I pray

And so it

Will be done

Odam!

Take the cord and place it in an appropriate place. This should be evident after the spell is done. It could be in front of the image of Lilith, at the crossroad, a desolate place, stream or graveyard. The whispers in the soul will tell you where.

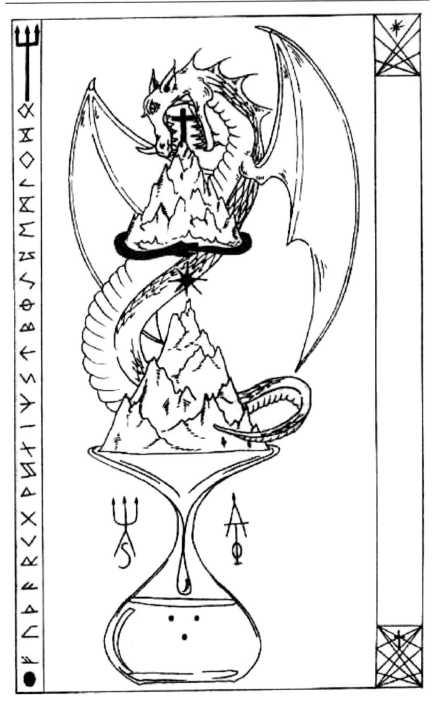

TRÉS CAMINHOS DO EXÍLIO VIA VERA CRUZ - BY AUDREY MELO

6

The Art of Timeless Tradition

"Know that the soul, the devil, the angel are not realities outside of you; you are them

Likewise, Heaven, Earth, and the Throne are not outside of you,

Nor paradise nor hell, nor death, nor life.

They exist in you; when you have accomplished the mystical journey

And have become pure you will become conscious of that."

-Najmoddin Kobrã

Today, in our modern world the word 'tradition' refers to anything handed down that rests on a real or assumed pedigree. A tradition can be something invented, a fantasy of a true transmission of Gnosis. The modern world insists on action and individualization, elements that in a 'traditional world view' are associated with regal powers and the warrior caste. Everything is mediated and measured in conformity with the norms of the warrior ethos. Thus is Modern Luciferianism understood and assumes the role of axis of the world.

From a metaphysical perspective, tradition isn't bound by any static philosophy or manifest social order. Tradition radiates from the sacred centre and replicates a certain order. This rests on the traditional tripartite order found everywhere in creation, which is between the center and its perimeters. The traditional world view is presented in the teachings of Plato. Here is a natural hierarchy composed of mind, soul and body. All traditional order adheres to this hierarchy. The colours black, red and white denote the tripartite division of the arts. The colour black is given to earth, what is bodily and manifest. The colour red is given to the soul and its vehicle, the passions. White, being the power of peace and contemplation belongs to the mind.

White is the absence of colours, and is therefore the potentiality of all manifestation. Red is the colour given to warriors and kings, who use the force of passion to protect and secure. Black is the colour of serfs, peasants and artists. In this hierarchy we see how the sacerdotal art, which is of an astrological and celestial nature informs the axis mundi. The warrior ethos represents the core of what is martial, namely alchemy. The 'black arts' make use of the earth, plants, animals, everything terrestrial. But all is related in its play back and forth to the celestial centre.

Allow me to explain this, from a Craft perspective. Those few times I have seen Janicot mentioned it is always as either a devil or as 'the black man of the Sabbath'. Neither of these assumptions is wrong, but it is a simplification. Janicot is never manifest, he simply is the sacred centre of 'the black arts'. The Sun and the Moon are his eyes. Janicot uses the luminaries to mark the perimeters of the art, just like the One uses them to mark the perimeters of the absolute. The witches through all times marked the limits of divine possibility and by this they gained the reputation of 'evil', just as the Muslim Iblis and the Christian Judas Iscariot gained a similar bad reputation.

Seeing the world form this perspective inevitably invites a dichotomy between the sacred and the profane, where a profane world perspective is represented by a view dislocated from traditional order. These considerations are important, because it places witchcraft within a traditional order. From this order the witch will realize the particular 'vinculum' he or she is operating from and be able to re-align the world of matter to the sacred centre. From this follows that 'spiritual realization' as something that occurs in conformity with the appointed station Fate gave to each one of us. Tradition as such flows from the living and dynamic celestial ray that awakens latent potentiality in the human being and calls them to their station. We find here an interplay between intellectual intuition (the supra rational), inspiration and revelation.

Traditional faiths have their exoteric dimension, defined by religious law. The predicament of the witch is the realization of two laws, of nature and of civilization. These laws are not in conflict, but are related to different forms of order. The laws concerning civilization, arise from natural possibility and are limited.

Relativism and eclecticism is widespread amongst contemporary Pagans, magicians and mystics. 'New traditions' see themselves as fractions of a traditional Craft lineage on the basis of selection of the available material and a unique or personal expression. The Latin word *traditio* means 'surrender' as well as something 'handed down'. Tradition can therefore be understood to be surrender to what is handed down. The Safed Kabbalists of medieval Spain understood tradition to be a reception, by prophetic inspiration of the kernels of Gnosis. This was only possible by ardent study and surrender to the 'Law'. The 'Law' or Torah is worthy because therein is found the word of God, spoken both plainly and allegorically. The Law was understood to be something everyone could adhere to. The way of adherence was motivated by the inclinations of the soul and the maturity of the mind.

When people or groups claim to be traditional but no such sensitivity is found, it is like walking alien landscapes with no compass and no solid knowledge about the terrain. The lack of knowledge and direction invites theories and hypothesis. Over time a pattern emerges, made by one's own confused steps and this is how 'modern traditions' come into being. These 'systems' cannot be 'traditional', rather they run counter to its transcendent aim. The importance of the transcendent and what is unmanifest is what makes tradition timeless and eternal. Established on traditional metaphysics and contemplative activity ascent and descent is possible and we can bring heaven on Earth.

The Goal and Core of the Wise

One traditional manual of magic and theurgy is the 9th Century magical manual *Picatrix*, or "The Goal of the Wise". This grimoire or *grammar* draws upon many influences that all accept a traditional world view. It is a compendium or primer of magical lore and techniques from many lands. Central in *Picatrix* is the knowledge of astrology. Astrology is basically a science explaining how we can manifest divine virtue on Earth. Its procedures and techniques, thoughts and talismans rest on a holistic, geocentric and Ptolemaic world view. The geocentric worldview is criticized because this is not how things are in reality. Ultimately it is all about what is effective and useful. Approaching situations from the perspective of an angel residing in the 6th heaven will not help us much here on Earth. To find our way we need to start from where we are, not from some ideal location. In the language of the stars, we need to orient our life from our own house and not that of our neighbour.

Natura Perfecta and the Talismanic Art

In the *Picatrix* we find a complete *nigromantic* manual for the talismanic arts. A traditional *nigromancer* or magus strives towards achieving the soul's perfection. This procedure for perfecting one's nature was given by

Hermes Thrice Wise via dreams. The author of *Picatrix* begins each chapter with a quote from Aristotle's *Astimech* thus: "Perfect nature strengthens he who seeks wisdom, firms his intelligence and wisdom, permitting him to succeed more easily in all his works."

The instructions in *Picatrix* inform us that this ritual was done once a year, and it is fair to assume that this was associated with one's day of birth when one's good *daimon* was especially close. The astrological observation calls for the Moon to be in the first degree of Aries, its "horns". As discussed in the first chapter, the horns of Aries were indicators of dominion and mastery. The stars in the horns of Aries are *Sheratan* and *Mesarthim*, which are of the nature of Mars and Saturn. We see here a reference to the great benevolence of Mars as God of pure spirit and Saturn as the King of the Golden Age. Communion with one's *Natura Perfecta* is symbolized by these two planetary forces.

Christopher Warnock comments in his book *The Mansions of the Moon* that the first mansion of the Moon signifies the Divine Mind (*nous*), primal transmission and the power of creation/destruction. And here is an enigma, the power that creates is also what destroys. This mansion was of great importance for the traveller, especially as the journey commenced. So, it would be right to understand the ritual for making contact with one's *Perfect Nature* as the beginning of a journey motivated by the Divine Mind. The composition of the horns of Aries also calls to mind how easy it is to lose one's way.

The ritual calls for a preliminary invocation done over a well. You should place a candle in a glass, so that the flames do not blow out and collect earth from the four sides of the well and its centre. To gain insight into the mystery of the world place yourself over the well with the talismanic substances and one single candle burning. I suspect that the position is on one's back turning the attention to the darkness above while you rest on the darkness of the earth and its secrets. Prior to this ritual use the earth or clay to make a talisman to stop the wind.

The ritual itself is quite simple, and can be done once a month. On the day that falls closer to your birthday it would be advisable to offer food, sweets, pie and flowers on a table and invite friends to partake of the delights.

Prior to the ritual make sure that the temple room is clean, dress the table with a clean cloth and take four bowls, filling one with real butter, the other with almond oil, the third with walnut oil and the fourth with sesame oil. Place them at the centre of the table with one beeswax candle lit in their midst. Then take four glasses and fill them with wine and place at each cardinal direction. Lastly place on the table a bowl with honey, sugar and flour.

Chant:

Meegius, Betzahuech, Vacdez, Nufeneguediz

You are the Wardens of Natura Perfecta

Come forth from the quarters of the heavens and

Sustain my ascent

Open the secrets of the World to me

And let me see my Self and the Journey onwards!

Meegius, Betzahuech, Vacdez, Nufeneguediz

Then take two censers and lit the charcoal saying:

Oh black as Saturn are you and by Saturn I expel all malefic forces from you

When the coal is red-hot say:

Hot as Mars are you, glowing with the Fire of the Divine Mind,

By Mars I expel all malefic forces from you

Then take frankincense and mastic and place in one of the censers and aloes wood in the other. As the smoke rises say:

Oh rise to the heavens, these vapors of fragrant ascent, rise to the Throne of God and make Sweet the Divine Mind and the journey onwards.

For you my Angel, My Perfect Nature I give this offering of scent and vapors, the Love of the World in aerial ascent!

Then face east and call upon *Natura Perfecta* seven times with the following petition:

"I invoke you, O spirits mighty, powerful, and lofty, because it is from you that proceeds the knowledge of the wise and the intellect of those who understand, and it is by your virtue that the requests of philosophers are manifested, so that you may answer me, that you may be with me, that you may link me to yourself by your powers and virtues, that you may strengthen me in your knowledge, so that I may understand what I do not understand, that I may know that of which I am ignorant, that I may see that which I see not; set far from me blindness, indignity, forgetfulness, and weakness; make me to climb to the degree of the wise ones of old - those who had a heart full of knowledge, wisdom, intellect, and savvy - fasten that in my heart in such a manner similar to the heart of the wise ones of old."

When this is done, mix the oils and butter in the bigger bowl and place it in the north. Combine these ingredients into a pie. Add some wine if needed and while the pie is being baked sit in contemplation enjoying the spirit of the wine and awaiting the descent of your Perfect Nature. Chant the names of the four elementals that guard the congress.

Alternatively in this phase you can also use the names Ibn Khaldun cites for calling upon the *Perfect Nature*. These names can also be substituted in their entirety for the ritual and are as follows:

TAMAGHIS - BA'DAN - YASWADDA -
WAGHDAS - NAWFANA - GHADIS
Finally consume some of the pie and give some to friends and neighbours.

The Perfect Nature and the Familiar Daimon

It is striking how similar the idea of the *Perfect Nature* is with the Socratic familiar *daimon* and the concept of *Orí* amongst the Yoruba of western Africa. Empedocles in the 5th Century BCE describes the *daimon* as being the true self. Heraclites said that a man's character is his *daimon*. Plato, expresses it best of all:

> *"...regarding the supreme form of soul in us, we must conceive that the god has conferred it upon each...as a guiding genius (*daimon*) - that which...lifts us from earth toward our celestial affinity, like a plant whose roots are not in the earth, but in the heavens".*

The concept of *daimon* and genius is the same. For the Romans the genius was understood to be a tutelary deity, just like the familiar *daimon*. The Latin root, *genere*, "to generate" describes the generative process and was understood to be an external and incorporeal extension of man, the spirit of his destiny. Socrates saw the *daimon* as companion and guide. Genius gave its name to the *genii* and is related to one's true character or mental capacity.

The psychologist Dr. Sanford asserts that the cooperation of the ego is required if the *daimon*/genius is to operate successfully. From the perspective of ego psychology, this makes sense. This divine aspect of personality may operate through the ego, whether it is aware of it or not. When we speak of one's *calling*, we refer to the fundamental character, orientation and activity of the ego. Similar ideas lie at the core of the wisdom tradition of the Yoruba. It might be helpful to look at the idea from this angle.

To Receive Oneself

Amongst the Yoruba the idea of self is intimately related to a connection between the material and celestial world. One might classify the Yoruba perspective as a dualism perceived as unnatural and consequently the goal is to undo this separation. The perceived dualism in the world is a flaw that we must mend.

The word of importance here *Orí* is often translated into the phrase "to receive oneself" as the words composition "O" signifies he or her and "rí" denotes to receive. It can also mean "head" or "summit". *Orí* is at the same time the physical head, as well as the spiritual quality associated with the head, its *àse* or power and ability. These qualities are first and foremost related to consciousness and also one's station in life. Without *Orí* nothing can be accomplished and no evolution can be made, no wisdom can be comprehended, nothing be understood. As the Yoruba proverb goes: *Eni t'ó gbón. Orí è l'ó ní ó gbón* or in plain language: "he who is wise, is made wise by his *Orí*."

Orí is at the same time man's consciousness, his physical head and also our most important *Òrìsá*. *Orí* brings to mind the "Guardian Angel" or Socratic *daimon* as it is one's personal protective deity. It oversees an individual's evolution and assists in his travel on Earth and the return to *Órun. Orí* is considered to be the most important, arcane, and ancient of all the deities created in *Órun*. Without consciousness there can be no perception. *Orí* is composed of the following segments.

1. *Orí ode,* which signifies the physical head.

> *i. Orí inú,* which signifies the inner head, this means consciousness, perception and our experience of identity and selfhood. The *Orí inú* is further segmented into two segments, *Apárí-inú* and *Orí Àpeere. Apárí-inú* refers to the seat of one's inner consciousness. This aspect of the consciousness is responsible for cultivating one's character, one of the most important tasks for our personal *Orí* to perform. Only by developing good character one can attract good fortune. The development of good character is intimately connected with being conscious. Ifá speaks of the importance of being conscious of the good and bad things that happen in life. Bad things serve to harden one's integrity and character. The lessons that life gives are a challenge and the way we conceive of these challenges makes the difference between developing good character or failing.

2. This idea is again related to another concept known as *Èrí okàn,* which means "the testimony of the heart". In *Ifá* this signifies that good consciousness is indispensable for good character.

3. The other concept *Orí ápeere* speaks about creation. For instance, the element of water remains the same element but takes on various forms within the clouds, ponds, under the Earth and within its creatures. This means that everyone exhibits a specific elemental feature depending on their constitution. This is related to the transmigration of souls.

Incarnation, transmigration and such terms naturally raise questions about death, afterlife and the nature of the soul. In this regard *Ifá* teaches that each soul was pre-existing. It is purely esoteric to speak of the elevation of selfhood through successive visits to the Earth. *Ifá* maintains that the invisible abode is our true home. This process of purification or elevation is called *Ìpònrì*. This word denotes the circle of incarnations (*atunwa*) and is related to the goal of our incarnations ending in *Àpeere*. This concept touches the heart of *Ifá* and speaks of one's destiny and character.

Destiny (*Ipin*) has two important aspects. *Àyànmó*, which is fixed and unchangeable and *Àkúnlèyan*, that can be changed. Good character is developed by honesty, humbleness, generosity, honour, wisdom and kindness. Good character is the source of all good things in life - especially wealth, prestige and prosperity. It is usual to consider a person that has achieved a good character to be cool-minded and calm in the face of joy and sorrow.

The *Orí* is the seat for character and mediator of guidance from the beyond. In addition there are also three centres where spiritual congress or possession by spirit is possible. These centres are:

Iwájú Orí a powerful center within the brow, where the "third eye" is found. This is the source for divine inspiration and for developing one's character.

Àtàrí is the centre found in the crown of the skull. In *Ifá* this centre is where one experiences the source of creation. One's being merges outside the confinements of time and space and enters into communion with the source. In this realm the wisdom of *Odù* (the energy patterns of creation) is retrieved and in made manifest by the diviner (*Babalawo or Awó*). During divination the *Awó* activates this centre and is said to return to the time when "Prophet of *Ifá*", walked the Earth and thus *àṣẹ* is released. This *àṣẹ* can also manifest in the form of vision and dreams as well as deep insight into the complexity of situations, aided by prayers, enchantments and poetry. It is a condition or state beyond intellectual and relativistic reality.

Ìpàkó signifies the point in the nape of the neck where our older brain is found. This point connects us to the variety of animal forms and also powers of nature, usually referred to as *Òrìṣà*. Mystical vision can also flow from this point. This centre is activated by prayers, songs, music and rhythm and facilitates possession by divine beings that enter the body and consciousness of the worshipper taking control of a person and using them as a medium. I hope, by going into such depth from such unexpected angle to throw some light on the mechanisms of witchcraft. From a Yoruba perspective man is a symbol of cosmos and all its potential.

The Point and the Circle

The Wheel of the Year and the Sabbaths are perhaps the hallmark of modern witchcraft. Clearly the observance of the turning cosmic tides, marked as the Sun enters the cardinal signs is important. Rituals to ensure rain, fertility of crops and such were important for agricultural societies and by extension those who depend on the fruits of the Earth. However the meaning of the circle as sacred space needs to be established in relation to the point or pole that marks the sacred centre. The polestar symbolizes the sacred centre as cosmic north, the dwelling place of the Hyperborean Apollo and the Hidden Imam.

The circle is defined in accordance with its centre. The same idea plays itself out with *Shiva* and *Shakti,* who represents the possibilities unfolding from the point. This formless centre is indivisible and a unity is in all senses. The point is the focus and the circle is the world it generates. To walk the circle is to observe the stages of the Sun as it moves in its natural sequence, widdershins, through the zodiacal signs.

Any circular form represents the celestial spheres and every square represents the Earth. The Masonic expression "squaring the circle" is a reference to bringing down heaven upon the Earth. This relationship between point, circle and Sun is evident from the alchemical and astrological symbol for the Sun, a point within a circle.

The cross in the circle marks the cardinal stations of the Sun's journey. The eightfold year generates the Rosicrucian symbols of the *Rota* or *Rosa Mundi*. This symbolism has striking similarities with the Athenian Horologium, or 'timepiece' . This tower for measuring time was erected circa 50 BCE by Andronicus of Cyrrhus. It was an octagonal structure also known as the Tower of the Winds. Each of the eight sides bore inscriptions dedicated to the eight winds: Boreas for the North, Kaikas for the North East, Eurus for the East, Apeliotes for the southeast, Notus for the south, Lips for the South West, Zephyrus for the West and Skiron for the North West. At the centre of the Tower is a water- clock and several sundials.

These eight winds are associated with the eight angels, in accordance with Psalm 104 - light is the centre and from this light, rays of fire and air are sent forth. Angels are "those who walked upon the wings of the wind". Eight is also important because of the eighth Kabbalistic *sephiroth (Chesed)*. This is the dwelling place of Seth, the perfected one and Abel's replacement. Agrippa related grace, misery, corruption and the in-corruptible to this number. To square the circle into eight parts is to generate the intermediate world, the meeting point between the terrestrial and celestial. The eight winds represent the passage from terrestrial and celestial world, just as the Rose represent the secret hidden within the Tower of the Eight Winds, or the Mystery of the Rose protected by eight angelic messengers.

This blending of the celestial and terrestrial is evident in contemporary Druidism, where a circle is made, usually with a portal and a square stone altar. This ritual symbolism strikes the axis from Heaven to Earth. In ritual one enters the sphere of heaven and focuses on the Earth as a point. The meaning of the stone is significant. The square black *Kaaba*-stone at Mecca or the Oygigigi of the Yoruba, are related to the cosmic centre. A stone on a burial ground is in truth the mountain of ascent. In function the stone is like the pole or axis connecting us to our ancestors.

The Compass and the journey of the Soul

The compass is not the circle; but a tool for establishing the spiritual direction. The magical squares of the planets can also be referred to as a compass. To strike a compass means to establish the sacred space, one's circumstances for generating the way of ascent. The point and the circle establish particular ways the sacred centre unfolds.

The compass is an instrument of navigation and orientation that points to magnetic North. The Muslim *Qibla* points to the spiritual North, at Mecca. The Masonic compass refers to the curved or crooked line that was the blueprint for the building. We should understand the word compass in a Craft sense to be the laying out of the blueprint that points onwards to the spiritual centre or Hyperborean realms. Even today this instrument of navigation is referred to as the compass *rose*. Sailors navigate by the stars and Polaris. This also represents the spiritual North, the *Lux Mundi*, where the light descends and calls us back to the original un-fallen state by means of the Ladder of Light.

The many feast days before and after the winter solstice, Sol Invictus, Saturnalia and Larentalia, function to create movement and prepare the ladder of return. This is also disclosed in the importance of *Ursa Major* or the Plough as the Bull of Heaven. These seven stars are also known as the seven poles of Heaven, the guardians of the Hidden Imam.

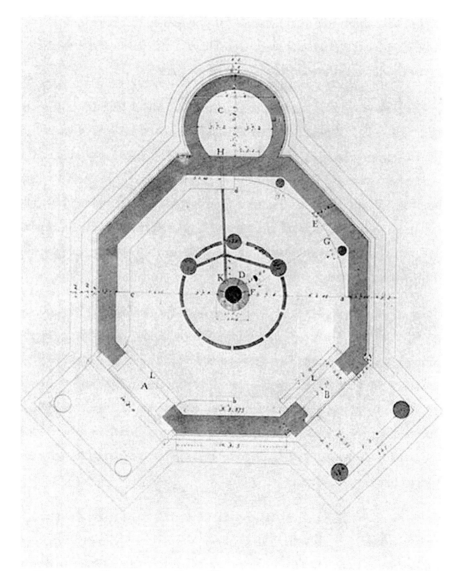

PLAN OF THE TOWER OF THE EIGHT WINDS WITH THE WATER CLOCK IN THE CENTRE.

The Plough has the significance of opening the way and also indicates the agricultural nature of the Craft, the arts of the countryside. In the Yule celebrations the Christmas tree has its crowning star. Yule shares the day of *Sol Invictus*, the cosmic law again reaffirmed, the light vault of the Hidden Imam as the point of the world.

We see here the traditional reasons for the eighth and northern quarter to be a gate of silence and darkness. Here at the gate of the world we access the un-manifested potentiality of all things.

In *The Pillars of Tubal Cain* Mike Howard and Nigel Jackson comment that: "The celestial pole is the secret behind the symbolism of the four-sided spinning castle of the witch Goddess. This turns eternally at the heart of heaven and is the gateway to Hyperborea, or the land beyond the North Wind. For the initiate of the Mysteries, Polaris is symbolically the sword point, the City of Enoch and Cain, the Iron Star, the Celestial Nail, and the stellar structure in the skull-dome of Heaven, the gateway to the Great Beyond".

The spinning movements of the Queen's castle disclose the Mystery of the Rose in the Tower of the Eight Winds. Lady Venus propels the spinning about the point. The circle guided by the nail star is set in motion and from the gate of silence the formless powers of light and unity are brought into being. As such the tower and its eight angels, the Rose Queen at its centre, becomes a design and a compass for the soul's journey home through the gates of becoming. It signifies a return to the Golden Age, to the City of Heroes.

North on the wind or compass rose is used to be marked by the letter T for *tramontina*. T is also the Tau cross or the Trident, the crossroad or witches' foot. In the 14th Century, Columbus replaced the T with a *fleur de lis*. To choose the image of a lily instead of the natural flower amongst thorns, might indicate the lunar quality of the Moon as mirror of celestial influences. The lily is not only a lunar symbol of chastity or virginity, but it is also a toxic plant from whence the word delirium is derived.

The Hebrew *lulav* made from palm fronds, myrtle and willow woods, that by tradition is ascribed to Venus and the Moon, is similar to the *fleur de lis*. Palm fronds carry multiple meanings ranging from what remains hidden and justice, to strength and uprightness. Throughout the Middle Ages the lily was held by virginal women in aristocratic or mystical marriages. Later Latin misspelling of fleur de lis as *fleur de luce*, flower of light, translate as being the spiritual light in the hand of the virgin.

The French hidden convent also made use of the *fleur de lis*. They were dedicated to the Mysteries of Luna as she ignites the power of shapeshifting and immortality in the Brotherhood of the Black Lily. This is replicated in the family's coat of arms: a wolf's claw around a pole inscribed with the word 'on', meaning light. The Black Madonna of Chestochowa is draped in a black cloak covered with golden *fleurs de lis*

The Rite of the Wind Rose

The rose and the compass are indicative of the soul's journey, the whirling tower of the Queen that lies at the heart of the eight winds. This rite is done either outside on the green grass or by a green altar-cloth on a square table. You will need nine roses and to fashion a witche's foot from willow, myrtle and whitethorn. Eight of them point to the directions, the blossom at the compass edge. Place the blossom of the ninth at the centre of the table on the witches' foot. Have a single lily to your left and a chalice of red wine to your right. Burn benzoin, rose and myrrh.

Fumigate yourself and the table well and leave the censer hanging in the north.

Now take eight candles, four white for each cardinal direction, and four red for the mid-quarters. Anoint them in olive oil and inscribe with a wooden quill, preferably made from a nut tree or whitethorn, the name of each wind and place them in their appropriate quarters. The centre may be dark or lit by an oil lamp.

You will then present your petition to the Queen by knocking on the table three times and saying:

Fair Queen who holds the great lights in her hands

I stand here in the wilderness of All to seek thy comfort.

Grant me access to thy kingdom

I am here with my heart in my hand

Coming from the ruddy fields to seek thy comfort

Then you turn to the north and see there an angel dressed in a heavy black cloth holding a twisted conch in his hand, call him by his name BOREAS.

Then turn to the northeast and see here an angel holding a shield decorated with many symbols of various kinds, call him by his name KAIKIAS.

Then turn to the east and see here an angel holding a clock filled with the abundance of the earth, fruits and grains and call him by his name APELIOTES.

Then turn to the southeast seeing here a mighty angel using as a shield his heavy cloth to defend against the elements and call him by his name EUROS.

Then turn towards the south and see here a gentle angel pouring out from his jar a river of fresh water and call him by his name NOTOS.

Then turn towards the southwest and see here an angel in the form of a boy-child who sustains the mast of a ship and holds the evil winds at bay, and call him by his name LIPS.

Then turn towards the west and see here a youthful angel with flowers in the hair and call him by his name ZEPHYROS.

Then turn towards the northwest and see here an angel with a bearded face holding a pot of bronze filled with hot ashes and burning charcoal, call him by his name SKIRON.

Allow yourself to see the Queen seated in the heart of the Rose, resting on the witche's foot and pray to the winds to guide your journey towards the Tower of the Eight Winds and let the eight angels lead you on your journey.

In conclusion I present an inspired rendering of the Gospel of Judas as it applies to the journey of the soul "against the current". It is common to see Cain as the ancestral Witch-father, but it is important to see his role in a greater design, as "the man who does what needs to be done". The role of Cain is similar to that of Judas Iscariot. The recently rediscovered *Gospel of Judas* is clearly useful as a compass in its own right, as it points the journeyman towards the Pole and sacred centre.

The Ordeal of Powers' Concealment

"For I am the voice that speak through your fear

I am the power that enters when you have no more"

From Liber Combusta, The Gospel of the Stellar Fire

The path presents four ordeals, each of them aimed towards self-mastery. The first ordeal is by Air, the second by Water, the third by Fire and the fourth by Earth.

Air can be a mighty wind fueling the waters to raise mighty in rage, for the fire to die and for the earth to vanish. The ordeal by the winds challenges our sense of separation, our mind, thoughts, thinking, goals, sense of identity. This is the nature of the ordeal of the wind, to stand strong against the challenges of the Devil and not let the waters rise, the fire die nor the earth erase our memory. What makes the path so hard is spoken of in the *Gospel of Judas*: "some walked in the way of righteousness while others walked in their transgression". The master is not speaking of a division between people in terms of bad and good. He refers to the estate of his followers, seekers in general whose hunger for the gardens of milk and honey outside the temple can only be quenched by transgression. Woe upon the pilgrim of the lonely road, woe upon the one who willingly takes the mark of the first sorcerer. Woe upon the accursed blood, for the curse is the holy work of salvation. By the deeds of Jezebel, Judas Iscariot, Delilah and Herodias shall the holy work of transgression be accomplished, so we may be righteous and stand forever.

Where there is no transgression there can be no salvation. The Devil is the first of air and he splits the winds four ways —causing confusion as to right and wrong. The air is the breath, what separates us from the corpse. Air is divine, so the ordeal is in this realization of the life sustaining air.

Of the second ordeal we read in the *Gospel of Judas*: "when Jesus observed their lack of understanding he said to them; 'why has this agitation led you to anger? Your god who is within you has provoked you to anger within your souls. Let any one of you who are strong enough among human beings bring out the perfect human and stand before my face.' "

A lack of understanding sets the waters in motion. This ordeal arizes from the she-devils, obscure caverns of dark lustful secrecy. Also the wounds of your soul and the scars on your heart. You might say, we are here speaking of control. For power uncontrolled is power wasted. It is this power the Devil challenges you to yield. And I say, give him not what is rightly yours! In this lies the curse and the kingdom. It is transgression by not succumbing to the demands of the moist darkness. In this is the oath and its foreswearing. Your heart must choose the dark or light. Where there is no heart there can be no love, without love no passion. As the mark is taken and the curse bestowed, a fire is kindled and the lonely pilgrim goes into the world as an outcast!

In the third ordeal the curse and its load feeds the lantern, your guiding light - as wind and water will extinguish it. Our ancestors referred to this stage as *rubeata*, the reddening of the profane - to invest it with holy fire. In this ordeal belief challenges our right to the holy fire. At each forked road the Devil forces you to demonstrate that you truly, by mind and heart, have penetrated the veils of ignorance, that you willingly and knowingly take on the curse.

Here is loneliness, or "one-liness", being ONE. We meet the silence of our belief, the flickering flame kindled in our heart that brings balance to the waters. This is the silence which we fill with our own doubts, insecurities and distractions. It is in the silence of fire that spirit speaks and we measure our worth. In the silence of fire there is no self-pity, no going back, no remorse, no forgiveness. You must become one or perish!

With thy lantern you walk the earth. The last ordeal is always what lies under our feet, the earth itself, and the mystical north. Her name is Foundation. And know this, oh journeyman of the accursed road, if you have no foundation the earth will swallow you as it did with Koran and his profane rebels when they challenged Moses and demonstrated the great failure of the test of fire. The failure of fire will bring the waters to vanquish the fire, the air to gather the dust of the earth – and by this your memory will be lost forever.

In the fourth ordeal the Devil will challenge you for the powers gained, you wrestle with your demons and the Djinns in a battle where you ascend or perish. By the holy transgression you will be named righteous. The Devil will be a companion and a beacon of undying light. Only by foundation will the gifts of Air, Water and Fire be sustained within the arms of the True Cross. Only thus can we station ourselves in the centre and take the horned skull of ancestry in our hands and say: "this is in my likeness, this black skull of our bloody beginning is rightly mine. I am the One from beginning to end. And so it shall be!"

Know pilgrim, that the way of power is the path of ordeal. In true power lies true mastery. We cannot have the one without the other. Mastering one's self and the transgression is a holy work leading to salvation. We can stand in the gardens of secrets in the courtyard of the Divine and feel the Divine breath. The mighty passion and the fire of inspiration rests upon a solid foundation. This is the legacy of holiness through ordeal. This is the exaltation of the wise blood. This is the straightening of the crooked road into a Ladder of Light for the ascent of the righteous ones, those who came out from the tribulation of transgression with the light of holiness blazing like a torch of victory in their hands!

But still, let the gospel of holy Judas Iscariot conclude the path of ordeal, for by each victory greater forces will rise from the servants of Saklas, not to challenge our victory, but to destroy.

"You will become the thirteenth,

and you will be cursed by the other generations —

And you will come to rule over them.

In the last days they will curse your ascent to the holy."

HANS HOLBEIN'S "THE DANCE OF DEATH".

DREAMS - BY AUDREY MELO

7

Within
the Veil
of Night

"The wild beasts of the desert shall also meet with the wild beasts of the island, and the satyr shall cry to his fellow; the screech owl also shall rest there, and find for herself a place of rest." (Isaiah 34:14).

"I am a brother to dragons, and a companion to owls." (Job 30: 29)

Few Mysteries are more misunderstood than those of the night. The greatest of these is related to the Jungian idea of the shadow with its assumed vaults of denied selfhood, staircases to some sort of divine ascent. The shadow has been subjected to societal punishment, steeped in moral judgements, particularly related to sexuality. The sexual finds its expression in the erotic, the aphrodisiac, the perverse and the more subtle nuances that speaks of attraction. Sex has become the illusory centre of freedom in which we find our shadow and the keys to unlock our shame and become free. By bringing the sexual to the light of day we manifest the most hidden caverns of self and the warrior ethos is played out. By conquering sexuality we attain a sense of freedom and the full glory of the individual. Forms of sexual revolt attack the moral constructs society and religion have imposed upon us for more than a millennium. But even with the heroic disclosure of sexuality, the sexual and erotic still holds a lure and mystique. This is the *Ars Veneris*, or "Venereal" Arts belonging to the realm of Venus as she rises to rule the night until dawn. In the Hymns of Orpheus Venus is praised *as* night.[29] When night spreads over the land, a different pulse takes over the world; draping it in a moist black cloth of unpredictability. The Sun has given her sceptre to the Moon, her moist and wild sister of changeability.

Spirits and deities of the night represent the powers of fear, the erotic and the unknown. The vampire transforms into a creature of the night under the caresses of Venus and Moon. Spirit tracks that under the Sun were desolate become alive. Night, when shapes change and the solar order rests. Poisonous vipers slide over the ground and birds, toads and bugs engage into a nocturnal symphony that soothes and scares. The night is the realm of dreams. Familiars and nymphs, fair folk and other spirits of the land commune with the dreamer in its caverns. The night belongs to Hekate as much as to Lilith. This is the time of spirits flying to feed on blood and semen in their mysterious work of restoration.

The Queen of the Emanations on the Left.

Lilith is one of the most enigmatic and misunderstood deities. Her form, function and reputation is misconceived and her knowledge lost. She has been overshadowed by the ideal of exalted womanhood, the chaste mother. Lilith represents untamed and free sexuality, used in Jungian psychoanalysis as the archetype for the vile sexual power within the murky roads of the psyche.

The Italian mage and philosopher Fulvio Rendhell is one of the few who lifted this veil revealing the mysterious 'Lilithian theme' as it unfolded from Mesopotamia up to our age. He makes clear that this power has a deep relationship with the Holy Spirit. The Holy Spirit reveals itself as a dove of peace but also as the terror of the night. These are contrasts and paradoxes. Lilith is the Holy Spirit as it descends by the power of the Moon and Venus. It is the *santa espirita nocturna.*

In the 10th Century *The Alphabet of Ben Sira Lilith* entered Jewish mysticism. This interest in Lilith was further disclosed in the writings of the Kohen brothers in the 13th Century and became part of the demonology of the *Zohar.* Thus was her role as "the mother of demons" and the progenitor of lewdness firmly established in Jewish mysticism. In modern psychoanalysis she is an archetype of the 'dark feminine' used to understand psychological processes as consequence of abuse. This is actually quite alien to her divine function. The Black Moon or Lilith has been given a wholly malefic interpretation. For me, this speaks about the difficulties we have in understanding the powers of night.

The identity of Lilith is revealed in the Old Testament *Book of Isaiah,* where she is referred to as a crooked serpent. Here also we find Lilith inhabiting deserted places and ruins and equated with the screech owl and the night hag.

Islamic lore reveals that she inhabits the same domain as the Djinns and, being fire, of the Holy Spirit. Just as fire can be a purgative, it also shares the nature of the Divine Mind. Fire can strike upwards or downwards, like the serpent fire in the body who rests coiled around the root. It strikes upwards to unleash enlightenment or downwards to ignite passion.

Contemporary analysts of Lilith's nature have fallen into two errors. The first is suggesting that the root of her name *lil* refers to the hostile spirits of the air, *lilins,* understood as malign rather than functioning in the divine design.

The other error is to associate her with "the shadow", as a form of all depravity, dislocated from a greater design and reduced to a function of the human psyche. Indeed, in the words of the Kohen brothers: "happy is he who understands these things as they are."[30]

The Lilithian theme stretches from Mesopotamia Ishtar into the fine veins of the world and gives its blood to Niritti and Bhairavi, to Hel and Freya, to the Mother of the Djinns and to the Holy Spirit. She is also Algol and Pleiades, she is Virgo and she is Venus, she is the power of cataclysmic possibility and she is the secret of immortality.

Skin leaping and the art of the undead

The Sabbath of the witches, night flight and their diabolic *orgia* in the shadow of time are ideas that followed the image of the witch. It is the fusion of the witch with the vampire. Since the Roman writers Apuleius and Ovid, the witch; *strix* or *striga*, or *strigoii* are similar if not identical beings, with their *varcolac*, roughly translated as wolf-coats. The Romanian term *strigele* refers to the ethereal lights found in forests and mountains, around trees of power and in caves. These lights are the fetch bodies of witches, either exorcised or convened in the Sabbath. Myths tell of nine spindles placed on the grave of the *strigoi*, as the power of the fates aided them and stopped them spinning the silver thread of night travel.

It is striking the relationship between vampires, wolves and witches found in myths all over the continent. These myths are particularly well preserved in Slavic regions. *Stregonis* were intimately linked to earth and air. In life they set out in the coat of the wolf, Saturn's beast, rising from his bed of moist cold earth and from the death like slumber in the shades of night. Upon death they went forth as bats and night-birds, especially owls.

This Mystery is explained by looking closely at Odinism. Fylgja (or fetch),

Hugr and Hamingja are the elements that make the esoteric anatomy of the vampire-witch A special band of warriors, *berserker*, were considered to be under the protection of Odin. They wore coats of wolf's fur, and were versed in the arts of *Seidr* (witchcraft) and *galdr* (enchantments). These arts were taught to them by Odin, patron of wisdom and wizardry. These warriors were those who died in combat and continue their battles in Valhalla. Each day they rise to battle, while in the night they sit at Odin's table eating the flesh of the pig Saerimne and the goat Heidrun. The warriors favoured by Odin, and picked by the Valkyries, are the bravest that died in battle. Odin prepares these warriors for the battle of the Gods at the hill of Vigrid. Some are taken to Folkvang, Freya's farm. This warrior band was "dressing their fetch" or fylgja, their animal familiar. Warriors were always considered to have a fylgja of an aggressive or fear-inspiring nature, such as wolf or bear. These special groups were brought together by their familiar, the *berserker* sharing the bear form and the *einherjer* sharing the wolf.

Ham or Hamingja, relates directly to the skin, veil or dress. The ability to change *ham* was considered a particular gift, providing fertility and related to hug or hugr the power manifested in Eros or Love. Hugr is understood to be a power possessed by sages and witches. The word denotes warm and passionate feelings of love and attraction. King Erik Aarsael of the Swedes who ruled for only one year from 1087 to 1088, was said to possess this particular power. He was the last of the heathen kings and became a symbol of luck with the ability to fertilize what was considered barren. Aarsael led the last *blot* in Uppsala and this gave him a strong relationship with the Vanir and Aesir, in particular Odin and Freya.

Legends of skinleaping, shapeshifting and lycanthropy are found everywhere in the world, from the jaguar allied *canaima* in South America to the were-boars of Turkey. These myths contain elements against the natural order, a consequence of some unavoidable event, such as the seventh child of a seventh child.

The minister Robert Kirk who wrote the *Secret Commonwealth* was the seventh son of a seventh son and it is curious that he reported intimate dealings with the Sidhe of the marshlands and hollow hills. The legends of King Lycaon, founder of Arcadia in the mountains of Greece carry all these motifs. Lycaon was the father of the muse Callisto and raised the son Nyctimus (night). Legend tells how Lycaon slaughtered Nyctimus and served this meat to Zeus who, repelled by the flesh of his own son, cursed Lycaon, turning him into a wolf. In Pausanias' version of the myth, Lycaon sacrificed a child on the altar of Zeus. Lycaeus (named after the event) and the child turned into a wolf. There are various explanations of this. Historian Robert Smith says that Lycaeus was the centre of a wolf-tribe in the mountains that usurped the sanctuary of Zeus. Other historians suggested that human sacrifice was given to Zeus who descends in the shape of a wolf.

Twelfth night runs from 26th of December to 6th of January: epiphany to the Saviour's baptism. This should be counted from the solstice and then twelve days, where each day is dedicated to one of twelve signs of the zodiac. This marked the end of the period starting with All Hallows, Halloween or All Souls Day.

The solstice is important for Sabbatic flight, as in contemporary revivals of witch cults. Actually, the solstices are those points when second sight is clearest, an excess of night in the winter and an excess of light in the summer. The cardinal signs Capricorn and Cancer, are at their peak, along with Saturn and Moon, earth and water, the very constitution of man.

In the *Homeric Hymn to Demeter* Hecate is called the *propolos* and *opaõn* of Persephone: her companion and guide. All deities with the ability to lead the descent to the Underworld such as Dionysius, Apollo, Orpheus and Hermes would be natural allies for the mastery of the necromantic and funerary arts.

By the 5th Century BCE. in Phrygia, Hecate is found in the company of Zeus and Cybele. Ausanias honoured her as "bringer of light" and in the city of Lagina she was honoured as *kleidos agõge*, "the processor of the key" – protector of cities and gates, hence the importance of the blade in her representation. In the City of Thasos, she was placed at each of the city's three gates and in Rhodes she was worshipped alongside Apollo and Hermes.

Over the decades Hecate transmogrified from honoured bringer of light and protector to mistress of ghosts and nocturnal outcasts, such as witches. This transition is partly explained by Hecate's role as patron of midwifes, maidens and virgins (unmarried women).

Hecate is found at the nocturnal crossroads, in boneyards and in association with *skia* or shadows, vile souls of the un-dead - angry ghosts. This vengeful class of ghosts called *alastõr* were intimately connected with early death and un-fulfilled destiny. Malevolent female ghosts threatened unborn children, as we see in the proliferation of amulets against them as well as *strix, lamiae* and *mormõ*. Hecate as gatekeeper, especially to the Underworld, naturally took on many of these vengeful and cold nocturnal aspects. Her grace and majesty lives on in her tripartite representation, with key, blade and torch, holder of the key, protectress and the light-bringer.

The three animals sacred to Hecate are the black sow, the mare and the bitch. Animals with second sight (dogs), which travel between the worlds (pig), bring nightmares (horse) and all related to fertility and lust. These companions and guides of Persephone are worthy icons for anyone travelling the Hel-way. The same animals are also associated with Odin, another traveller of the in-between.

Vampires are beyond time and space; they live in a perpetual eternity. Blackthorn is their nature and whitethorn is their bane and end. The stake that ends the life of the un-dead is rosewood or whitethorn. Legends from all over the continent tell of the protective use of garlic, poppy and thorns. Likewise fishnets and knots ward off vampires. They are either restrained by the knots or forced to untie them before wandering on. Thorny bushes and roses are said to protect against undesired visitations. Spirit tracks always follow straight lines, which is why in Brazil it is still the custom of funeral processions to following the crooks and hooks of the road. It is considered an ill omen for the deceased to be taken to the cemetery by the straight road, as this will leave a track for the un-dead to resurrect and return to torment the living.

The Power of the Moon

The Moon has a profound association with the Mystery of night. Her waxing and waning is of great importance for the ebb and flow of all fluids on Earth, water or blood. The Moon mediates all stellar rays, particularly by night. The Moon, the mother of pearls is associated with vampires and the un-dead. Agrippa comments in *De Occulta Philosophia*:

"And those things which are of like nature, as monstrous blood, of which are made wonderful strange things by magicians; the civet cat also changing her sex, being obnoxious to diverse sorceries, and all animals that live in water as well as on land, as otters, and such prey upon fish. Also all monstrous beasts, such as without any manifest seed are equivocally generated, as mice; which sometimes are generated by coition, sometimes of the putrefaction of the earth."[31]

The Moon is related to the power of traversing between the realms. Any abnormality related to water and blood is under its power. Likewise, the wonder-working properties of menstrual blood is a reference to generation by putrefaction of the earth. In Slavic vampire tales they frequently fly to the full Moon colouring it red in their hunger. It is by the full Moon that the skinleapers change into their familiar forms. Insanity rages high at this time and influence all living beings with ecstasy and lust. She moves through her gardens of different qualities during the lunar cycle of 28 nights.

In the *Picatrix* there is a formula for enticing the Moon and requesting her favours. One should dress in the manner of a young boy, place a silver ring on your finger and perfume the working area with pleasant aromas. Your petition should be presented in an eloquent and ornate fashion on the 14th day of the Moon's journey when she is free from malefica and positively aspected. The reference to the 14th day is most likely a reference to the 14th mansion *Al Simakh* found in the last six degrees of Libra and first four of Scorpio, a mansion that is related to the fixed star Spica, which has the nature of Venus. Spica is benign and such an aspect between the Moon and Venus will generate wonderful possibilities. The *Picatrix* says you should wash yourself in scented water and turn your face towards the Moon saying:

> "*May God save you, Luna, O Mistress who is happy, fortunate, cool and moist, even and beautiful. You are the head and the key of all the other planets, light in your movements, you who have a scintillating light, mistress of happiness and pleasure, of goodly speech, of*

*excellent reputation, of fortunate kingdom. You are she who loves
religion, who meditates upon the things of the world, full of subtlety
in your thoughts. You love and cherish pleasures, songs, and
pleasantries, mistress of ambassadors and envoys,*

skilled at revealing the Mysteries.

*You are free and priceless, you are for us nearer than
the other planets, you retransmit their light; by your bounty you
improve them, whatever be their state. Everything in the world is
beautiful when you are beautiful, and turns to evil when you are
turned to evil. You are the beginning of things and their end. You
have more nobility and honour than all the planets. This is why I make
to you this request.*

*And I conjure you by Celan, the angel that God has placed with you to
manifest all your effects, to have mercy upon me, to accept my
request, and by the humility that you have towards our Lord of
greatness and towards his reign, to make a good reception to me in
what I ask of you and for that which I petition you.*

*I invoke you by all your names: Camar (al Qamar) in Arabic, Luna in
Latin, Mehe in Phoenician, Zamahyl (Semele) in Greek, Cerim in Hindu,
Celez in Roman, in order that you grant in this place my requests."*

The supplicant is then to prostrate himself and offer to the Moon incense
made from mastic, cardamom, juniper, storax, cinnamon, myrrh and
twenty-two other ingredients, apples, wine and pine nuts. There follows
a lunar remedy that can serve as a *Vinum Sabbati.*

The recipe is as follows:
Laudanum, St. Johns Wort, apple, roses, grape seeds, pumpkin seeds, lily

root, dandelion root, spikenard and saffron, juniper and cinnamon, steep this in wine, put aside for two weeks, strain and let rest for the next time the Moon moves into the 14ᵗʰ Mansion.

Sol Niger & Luna Nigrans

To comprehend the darkness you must become night. The mercury of the philosophers must be brightened by the radiant sulphur until all that is left are the white bones of matter. At this point a new Sun dawns and the oceans of silver flow freely and en-soul the bones covered in eagle feathers. The Mystery of the "Lion's" blackening is radical as is the dryness of the silver. Many go wrong and the putrefaction turns to rottenness, the vessel breaks and the foul mixture corrupts the path. The child does not see the crown, the lakes of night are forgotten in the dragon's fight. The valley of the lilies is lost and the fountain is nowhere to be found. Many seekers of the Sun, the Moon and the Mystery of night surrounding the Black Sun and the Black Moon are lost in a pool of self-delusion and misconceptions. The mystery is simple for those who see with the soul, with the blackening of the Sun the waters flow freely into its garden. It is a release and a return. It is the becoming through ordeal. It is the Mystery of the path becoming the double-headed serpent and the Lady of milk.

The belief that the Black Goddess is our hidden and suppressed emotional life or unrestrained eroticism is delusion. Turn your soul to the north and from the land of power draw the flame of silver. You will see the green and the red enthroned in the castle of silence and there the flowers shall blossom. To understand darkness, the darkness must be realized for what it is, the fabric of creation, the fire of need and the glowing coals of veiled Mystery. This is the first realization of the path of silver. For the darkness is the nocturnal silver, moist and cold.

This mystery is in popular psychological terms referred to as something pertaining to the subconscious. I say that the Mystery of the silver night is *supra* conscious. It is the urge or drive denied by the conscious mind. We must look outside to the connectedness of all things and not within our own fragmented and veiled psyche. The modern psyche is a product of belief in our own greatness and lack of spiritual connection. Spiritual beings and the natural world are seen as something that dwells in the psyche. Man's psyche is released by Eros, a microcosm in itself. Only a man of love and soul can attract the natural and celestial sympathies. A person wrapped up in his own psyche and man-made world will attract the construction he lives within. And the Dark Goddess and the Black Sun become mere perversity and suicide. Only from the temple of Venus, forged in Psyche and Eros bond can the Seeker realize the radical paths against the grain. This is the eternal return, the dream made flesh.

Robert Graves said in 1964: "The Black Goddess is so far hardly more than a word of hope whispered amongst the few who have served their apprenticeship to the White Goddess. She promises a new pacific bond between man and woman, corresponding to a final reality of love… She will lead man back to that sure instinct of love which he long ago forfeited by intellectual pride."

The Black Goddess is Earth, and wisdom. She is the river of silver flowing over the blackness of the Earth. She is Ishtar who after seven steps stands naked in the halls of death to meet her fate. She is the Holy Spirit, giver of wisdom. She is the power and spirit released in sacred and sexual communion (maithuna).[32] She is the star of all sacraments, that summons us to the left path.

So, prepare for the coming of the Queen. The king must fall down at her feet, take on the wings of crows, to the touch of splendour. The Sun is reborn and the blackness integrated for the sake of love. The Sun is your "Ego". St. John of the Cross called this the dark night of the soul, putrefaction in the dragon's vessel wherein is brought all falsehood and selfishness. This is the secret of the north, where power resides. Dare to approach power in its pure form but journeyman be warned, the path has spikes and obstacles. The Black Goddess is no shameful sexual urge. She is the black light beyond the Emerald Castle and to reach her you must go beyond self. The way involves the blackening of the Sun, the annihilation of identity. The darkness seeps in like silent sharks and birds of prey. When the ego takes precedence one feels death and despair, a sense of losing yourself. By losing yourself you are found. By the blackening of the Sun, love enters although the return is painful. Love is the three coals that light the way.

It is sometimes said; she is a vampire, a sexual predator, a killer of children and a thief of semen. That she brings suicide into the heart of men. For some she is mercy and love, but for those who mistake mercy for folly and love for something crude, they will reap a bitter harvest. A harvest of seduction and rape, of lust and degradation – all in the name of failure and chaos.

The Black Goddess is the putrefaction needed to rejuvenate the Soul. The Black Goddess brings night into your soul, she covers you softly with claws and fangs, and when she asks one last time if you are ready to confront the northern night in all her awe, what will be your answer? The night is cold and moist and only with abandonment will you find what you need to survive.

A Rite for calling the Silver Guide in the Night of the Dragon

You must observe the heavens and see that the head of the dragon is in good aspect to a dignified Moon. The Sun must be neither dignified nor afflicted and most of all, the tail of the dragon must not swipe the house of death. The best conditions are Moon in Taurus. Go to a lonely place during the dark of the Moon, for it is then she bestows her virtue, breath and mercy. Draw a triskelion with bone powder mixed with grains of silver and sit down in the centre, facing north. To your left light a black candle and to your right a white. See yourself in the following way:

Your hue is golden, like the Sun but internally you see darkness and nothingness. Having established this visualization, allow your golden hue to turn black and broken. You are of the nature of night. Take a cup of red wine in a silver vessel and pour it upon the ground in the north saying:

> Oh great Dragon of the North
>
> May thy head look upon me in this night of rejuvenation
>
> Dragon who gives hope
>
> And opens the road to the Mountain of Venus
>
> I praise thee with your black hue and crowns of silver light
>
> I praise thee, old one who can secure the return
>
> And I call thee by my silence

You will see the Dragon appear from out of the darkness, make your mind receptive but do not create and anticipate the image. Use a scrying ball or mirror.

When manifestation occurs continue as follows:

The Door has been opened by the Old Dragon's kiss

The Night is upon me and I call thee from within

Holy Spirit of the North, Black One of the North

Claw handed and goat footed

By your wings and talon I call thee

Nameless One, by Bereshit I call thee

By the Forgotten Names I call thee

By the Spirits of the Air I call thee

By the Dragon's head and the Moon's embrace I call thee

Take another black candle and anoint it with ylang-ylang oil. Take off your clothes. Place them with your candle at the northern gate. Sit naked in the triskelion. Focus on the candle flame and say the following prayer:

I am what I am, a homeless Soul

I am what I am, Matter and Spirit

I am what I am and I shall become my Fullness!

This skin I offer to the night

This flame I offer to the spirits of the night

And I say, hear me; ye spirits

For I need ye

To intervene so I can reach the throne of your Queen

The Queen of the Night, I beseech thee!

I pray to thee

I call upon thee

I am a lost Soul calling upon Love

I pray that you in your Mercy

Release Love upon me

I seek the union of All

Teach me

That born from the old skin

I give to thee

Your blessings I ask

My gift is my own essence

And this token I give

For this oath

Sacrifice something from yourself, saliva, tears, blood, semen or vaginal fluids or your ecstasy. At the moment of sacrifice visualize the starry and Moonless sky assuming the form of a beautiful woman with a crown, wings, bird's feet and claws. If ecstasy is your offering focus during the stimulation and at the peak of ecstasy lie down and embrace her in your mind's eye. In receptive meditation wait for the Queen's arrival.

A complete sense of abandonment is necessary; it might seem simple, but can conclude in dramatic ways.

The ritual is closed in the following way:

Recite Psalm 22: 1-15. Give an offering of wine to the left and the right, extinguish the candles and in the darkness say:

I have approached thee

Lead me on the Path towards the union of Soul with Love

I am yours in for the sake of my wholeness

Teach me and temper me

Let me be grounded to do my work

Because under ground I can do nothing

I must be on the ground

Bless me so that I shall succeed in conquering myself

This is my prayer to the night

This is my cry to the Queen of Witchblood

This is my will to return

Bring me from the womb

Like a phoenix from the fires

May the coal of Love set my Soul aflame!

Amen! Amen! Amen!

This rite should be done at each dark Moon for nine months. Monitor your life carefully in light of the rite's purpose and the Mystery it conceals. In this rite lies the key to immortality. In this rite lies doom and redemption. In this rite lies love, mercy and its reflex, self-sacrifice and all shades of death.

Lilith - by Audrey Melo

8

Against the Current

To the sinful and vicious I am evil;
But to the good – beneficent am I.
-*Mirza Khan*, Ansari

Throughout history the witch has sat in the hedge, a position that gives a different view upon human activity. From her hedge the witch, views the world from the outside, one foot in the visible and another in the invisible world. One foot walks the path of the Sun and the other that of the Moon. From a profane or material perspective this defies mundane order; such a person moves with equal ease in several spheres, refusing to conform to societal demands, easily viewed as suspect. In our modern world the witch is not judged on the basis of superstition and fear, but by his or her ability to conform.

There is often an element of rebellion in the witch. This is caused by two things. One is the suppression of the people by the clergy because of their assumed possession of 'unholy' power. The patriarchal dominance in the world has made woman especially vulnerable to these accusations. The witch is sexual and erotic things and thus can be viewed as vile and mischievous.

Witches possessed the second sight, they saw both worlds simultaneously.

That of the Moon is the natural world where nostalgia for a return to nature was signified by a longing for a 'Golden Age'. As such 'witchcraft' is a poetic reality that breathes the vapours of the Moon and whose heart beats with the rhythm of night. "Going against the current" is embodied in this nostalgia, a rebellion against the world.

For Christians, the magical arts were problematic, blurring the boundaries between holy and unholy? The historian Kazhdan concludes that: "Unholy magic causes death, confusion, sexual misbehaviour; [whereas] holy miracles are creative, healing, and reviving."[33] And herein lies the ambiguity, something holy like a crucifix, could be infused (or used) with powers both pure and impure and used for holy and unholy ends. It was this ambiguity of cursing and curing that led to the witch being viewed with antagonism, fear, love and at the same time respect. The truth however, is that the witch was alienated from vulgar society and sought solitude and contemplation. She rebelled when disturbed. If we look at only two famous witches, Circe and her niece Medea, we see this pattern. In addition to a life of solitude and contemplation there is a vibrant relationship with the Sun and the powers of Venus. They are both *venifici* or herbalists, murder and love following in their footsteps. They are children of the Sun, daughters of Venus and the Moon respectively.

Circe – Regina Nymphae

Circe was a regal Goddess, married to the king of the Sarmantians, whom she poisoned. She was the daughter of Helios, and the sea-nymph Persea. By extension granddaughter of Poseidon – and thereby she had a natural affinity with the Sirens, the dreadful beings of utmost beauty and danger against whom she warned Odysseus and his men. She is of divine parentage and carries the Fairy blood of her nymph-mother.

Circe means 'falcon', a reference to the predatory flight of her fetch. Her pedigree was royal, and derived from Greek kings, especially of Colchis. As we saw earlier, the divine origin of witchblood is from Schemesh, the Sun. The Luciferian awakening is the phosphorescent radiance from the torch of the Sun. From Circe comes shapeshifting, the ability of transformation into an animal. She was also a *venifica* or poisoner. Circe's knowledge of drugs, plants, cures and poisons were her most poignant feature.

She lived a secluded existence on an island called Aeaea, also the abode of Helios, lions and wolves; animals associated with Lilith. Homer tells how Circe captured Odysseus' men, keeping them drugged at an eternal banquette. Hermes helps Odysseus, revealing to him the secrets of the herb *moly* (a herb known as 'snowdrop' or lily of the valley). This herb of the witch recurs in several Greek myths. It is related to mistletoe, the herb that took the life of the Norse *aesir* Balder.

Subtle references to Circe as sexual predator are reinforced when Odysseus, in spite of Hermes protection, becomes Circe's intoxicated lover for a year. Their three children became monarchs; viz Latinus and Telegonus of the Etruscans. Their daughter Aega was born from the Ocean and lived within a shield of ice.

Circe transformed Scylla, Glaucus' beloved, into a six headed monster. Her association with waters makes her a lunar Goddess, also a daughter of Venus formed in the image of Ishtar.

Medea - Granddaughter of the Sun

Accounts of Medea date back to at least 6th Century BCE. In them we see the impact of love and the ways of Venus. Medea's father, King Aietes offends Juno and who as revenge brings Aphrodite who with Eros' aid, causes Medea to fall hopelessly in love with Jason. She uses her witch-powers, inherited from Circe, to aid and protect Jason in his quest for the Golden Fleece. Medea enlists Hecate's help to protect Jason. Hecate enchants the dragon who guards the fleece and when Jason and his Argonauts land on Crete, the spirits of death are called to overpower Talos.

Medeas' father sends his half-brother Apsyrtos to bring her back. The lovers ambush and kill Aspyrtos. This senseless act of cruelty infuriates Zeus and Circe, who turn their back on her. Medea encounters the daughters of the recently deceased King Pelias, Jason's uncle, whom she promises to rejuvenate if they feast upon his flesh. The murder of Pelias was part of a greater plot by Jason and Medea. From this incident arises the cannibalistic accusations aimed at witches.

The lovers go to Corinth and experience ten years of happiness until Jason falls in love with Glauce the daughter of King Creon. Medea exacts a horrible revenge, sending a beautiful robe to the bride that consumes her with fire, killing all her children.

In Euripedes tragedy Medea next marries the Athenian Aegus. After attempting to poison Aegus, she leaves Athens to return home. Misfortune followed Jason until his death. Some accounts say he took his own life when he learned of the death of his children. Herodotus says that Medea was the indirect cause of the Trojan War, providing justification for the abduction of Helen. Legend tells that Medea migrated to Persia and that the Aryans changed their names to Medes in her honour.

The Icon of the Witch

Divine descent via Sun or Venus and Fairy blood come together in the image of the witch where 'the other side' opens up in ordeals and spiritual gifts.

Amongst the Babylonians Ishtar was the divine incarnation of the planet Venus. Venus was a deity both of love and war; a courtesan deeply associated with sexuality. One of her sacred cities, Erech or Eryx, was famous for the courtesans of the Goddess and for temple prostitution. This is also expressed in the name *Venus Erycina*, patron of prostitutes and all forms of "impure love". Ishtar was the courtesan of the Gods drunk on the ecstasy of the sensual. Lion pillars, like those of Lilith, stood at the entrance to her city. The Lion represents the Sun and the royal star at the heart of constellation Leo. Ishtar was daughter of the Moon-God Sin and in Harran influenced the Sabaean cult. As she entered the Underworld on the journey to challenge its Queen seven pieces of cloths are lost. Ishtar's famous "Dance of the Seven Veils" is related to the Mysteries of the seven planets and her dominion over them.

As in the case of Circe and Medea, Ishtar's love was a fatal drug. In Aphrodite, Astarte and Freya, love and cruelty are depicted in similar ways.

It is from these early representations that the image arises of the witch as unruly seductress, a poisoner, a hedonist, and social recluse veiled in mystery. It remained so until Jules Michelet's romantic presentation of the witch in *Le Sorcière* appeared in the 19th Century. In this work Michelet used his historical insight to paint a highly poetic image of the witch, similar in vein to his British contemporaries, Lord Byron, John Keats and Percy B. Shelley.

There are a few important characteristics that define the nature of the witch:

- We speak of a special pedigree, of someone with a solar seed, whose blood is partly from the other side. This gives access to secrets only revealed for those who possess the second sight and 'the mark'. A genuine connection with the formless truth of the source. This is seen in the witch's ability to converse with spirits and their vast knowledge of herbs for blessing or bane.

- The witch is a liminal being who must be connected to nature in order to feel content and complete. The degeneration of the natural world into a civilized and orderly moral universe of illusion induces resistance. The witch appears as someone standing still in the face of progress. In truth this is a rejection of the crooked ways of progress and insistence on the sacred centre and a return to the Golden Age.

- The Golden Age was a time of freedom, before law and the idea of *civilis*. Hence this path against the current and back to source often takes the form of lewd, immoral and shameless behaviour, but always with purpose and wisdom.

We must understand the witch as a being of nature. Witchcraft is the Venus-Craft of the countryside. Constant communion with the Fairy realm as well as the knowledge and wisdom of nature's gifts is typical of witchcraft. To remain in nature and maintain the legacy of the Fairy folk provokes those who see 'civilization' as good.

Even today, the country dwellers or *paganus* enamour, charm or provoke modern man by their love of wildness, the freedom of woods and springs, rejecting morals and profane law, in favour of the freedom given by Venus and the nymphs. Herein we find the true secrets of witchcraft, natural freedom and the realization of oneself as a fair being. And in this way she or he in her lewd lawless insistence on freedom is a mirror and a living critique of progress and law.

DRACO - BY AUDREY MELO

Farewell

And here is our journey's end. I have presented a living world among the stars, a land beyond the crossroad of change and fate, filled with aromas and virtues. Also a call, often neglected, to cultivate our perfect nature, the crucial axis of power under the Sun and Moon, resting in the hedge between night and day.

This book presents the main avenues of traditional witchcraft as I have synthesized them. This synthesis is born from my apprenticeship to a great variety of Craft lineages from around the globe. These expressions of Venus, or witchcraft, are all related to night and the liminal. Witchcraft is the poetic annihilation of the solar in favour of the magical order of the otherness of the night. In the night Venus is Queen in Heaven as the Moon is Queen on Earth as the left eye of God. As a nightwalker the witch makes herself receptive to dreams, visions and prophetic rapture. The goal for the witches' art is to understand how the invisible powers rule and regulate matter. Thus are things understood and manipulated.

The witch mediates between the white, or sacerdotal and the Black Arts of the Earth. And it is from this juncture rises the ambiguity of the witch. The witch's God has two eyes, the Sun and the Moon. God's watchful gaze at night and day. The infamous Devil joins the game, setting the limits and borders by virtue of choice. The witch will be balancing these things, understanding the solar world whilst thriving in the lunar waters as they flow over the Earth.

The Devil is the border of possibility, and the witch has for his or her playground the whole of manifestation from the solar pole to the diabolic abyss of the otherworld.

The witch lives at the crossroad of transcendence and manifestation. This challenges the ordinary world through gnosis or wisdom. The witch is a lover of wisdom, the arcane "natural philosophy" is her domain. The witch walks between the worlds, open for congress with the Fairy realm –the other side.

The witch is bound to no dogma. This makes them a threat to a Christianity established on doctrine. The witch insists everything in creation has its place. The Church insisted on two contrary substances God and the Devil. The witch strives for synthesis.

The moral dimension touches on piety and sexuality, seen by some as opposites. This conflict arose between *naturis* and *civils*, in certain taxonomies the wild and unpredictable versus the cultivated and ordered. The witch sought knowledge of good and evil in order to transcend, but dogmatic Christianity upheld a profane distinction between good and evil. The witch is perceived as evil by the evil but good by the good. In the role of fate and the Devil we may understand the diabolical accusations. As Devil the witch presented choice –a mirror for whoever sought her out. The witch is the moon reflecting your soul. If you dislike one you see, who is to blame?

The Greek national poet Kostes Palamas shall have the last word:

We are neither Christians nor Pagans,
With Crosses and pagan symbols
We are trying to build the new life
Whose name is not yet known

TOAD DEMON - AUDREY MELO

Selected Bibliography

Anon. (2005). Kyrandies. *On the Occult Virtues of Plants, Animals &
Stones*. Renaissance Astrology Facsimile Editions. US

Anon. (2002) *Ghayat Al Hakim. Pictarix*. Ouroboros Press. Seattle. WA

Ankarloo, Bengt & Clark, Stuart (2002). *Witchcraft and Magic in Europe*.
Penn. Pennsylvania. Six volumes.

Agrippa, Henry Cornelius (1531/1993) *Three Books of Occult Philosophy*.
Llewellyn. US

Best, Michael R. & Brightman, Frank, H. (Ed.) (1973). *The Book of
Secrets of Albertus Magnus*. Oxford University Press. Oxford

Bonatti, Guido. (2007) *The Book of Astronomy*. Cazimi press. USA

Briggs, Katharine (1978) *The Vanishing People: A Study of Traditional Fairy
belief*. Batsford Ltd. London.

Bruno, Giordano (1998). *Cause, Principle and Unity*. Cambridge
University Press. UK

Burkert, Walter (1987) *Ancient Mystery Cults*. Harvard University Press.
London

Burkert, Walter (1995). *Greek Religions*. Harvard University Press. UK

Cassirer, E, Kristeller, O, Randall, J.H. (1948) *The Renaissance Philosophy
of Man*. Chicago university press: US

Cavendish, Richard (1967). *The Black Arts*. Perigee Books: NY

Christian, Paul (1963). *The History and Practice of Magic*. The Citadel Press: NY

Churton, Tobias (2007) *The Magus of Freemasonry*. Inner Traditions: Vermont

Cochrane, Robert & Jones, Evan John (Ed. Mike Howard). 2001.*The Roebuck in the Thicket*. Cappall Bann: UK

Cristiani, Mgr. L. (1959) *Satan in the Modern World*. Barrie & Rockliff. London

Crowley, Aleister. (n.y.)*Goetia. The Lesser Key of King Solomon*, Sut Anubis. London

Davies, Owen (2003). *Cunning Folk. Popular Magic in English History*. Hambledon & London. UK

Duffy, Eamon (1992). *The Stripping of the Altars. Traditional Religion in England 1400-1580*. Yale University Press. London

Faivre, Antoine (1995) *The Eternal Hermes*. Phanes Books. US

Fries, Jan (2003). *Cauldron of the Gods. A Manual of Celtic Magick*. Mandrake of Oxford. UK

Frisvold, Nicholaj, de Mattos (2009). *Arts of the Night*. Chadezoad publication: Brazil

Ginzburg, Carlo (1991). *Ecstasies. Deciphering the Witches' Sabbath*. Penguin. NY

Grant, Kenneth (1975). *Images & Oracles of Austin Osman Spare*. Fredrick Müller. US

Heelas, Paul (1998) *Religion, modernity and postmodernity.* Blackwell. UK

Hellemo, Geir (1999) *Guds billedbok.* Pax forlag. Oslo. Norge

Huson, Paul. 2004. *Mystical Origins of the Tarot.* Destiny Books.

Hutton, Ronald (1999). *The Triumph of the Moon.* Oxford University Press. UK

Jackson, Nigel (1995). *Compleat Vampyre.* Capall Bann. UK

Jackson, Nigel (1996). *Masks of Misrule.* Capall Bann. UK

Kieckhefer, Richard (1997) *Forbidden rites.* Penn State Press. Pennsylvania

Kittredge, George Lyman (1929) *Witchcraft in Old and New England.* Oxford University Press. London.

Liddell, W. E. & Howard, Michael *The Pickingill Papers*, Capall Bann 1994

Lindblom, Johannes (1973) *Prophecy in Ancient Israel.* Fortress Press. UK

Maguire, Henry (ed.) (2008). *Byzantine Magic.* Dumbarton Oaks: US

Martin, Luther, H. (1987) *Hellenistic Religions. An Introduction.* Oxford University Press. Oxford

McGrath, Aliester E. (1997) *Christian Theology. An Introduction.* 2nd ed. Blackwell. UK

Michelet, Jules (1992). *Satanism and Witchcraft.* Citadel Press: NJ

Middleton, John (1678). *Practical Astrology. A Complete Guide to Horary Astrology*. Renaissance Astrology Facsimile Editions. US

Murray, Margaret (1921) *The Witch-Cult in Western Europe*. Oxford University Press. UK

Naudon, Paul (2005) *The Secret History of Freemasonry*. Inner Traditions. Vermont

Oberhelman, Steven, M. (1991). *The Oneirocriticon of Achmet*. Texas Tech University Press. US

Patai, Raphael (1990) *The Hebrew Goddess*. Wayne State University Press. Michigan

Qurra, Thabit Ibn (2005) *De Imaginibus*. Renaissance Astrology. USA.

Reuchlin, Johann. 1983) *On the Art of the Kabbalah*. University of Nebraska Press. London

Scot, Reginald (1584). *Discoverie of Witchcraft*. London.

Swartz, Michael, D. (1996). *Scholastic Magic*. Princeton University Press. New Jersey

Shah, Idries (1956). *Oriental Magic*. Arkana Books. NY

Smith, Meyer W. & Smith, Richard (1999). *Ancient Christian Magic*. Priceton. New Jersey

Stephens, Walter (2002) *Demon Lovers*. University of Chicago Press. Chicago.

Summers, Montague (1945) *Witchcraft and Black Magic*. Rider & Co. London

Sussol, Max (1995). *O Livro dos Benzimentos Brasileiros*. DCL. SP.

Taylor, Thomas (1986). *Iamblichus' Life of Pythagoras*. Inner Traditions: Vermont

Thomas, Keith (1971) *Religion and the Decline of Magic*. Penguin. New York

Thorndike, Lynn (1929) *A History of Magic and Experimental Science*. The Macmillan Company. NY Volume I and II

Tillyard, E.M.W. (1942) *The Elizabethan World Picture*. Vintage Books. NY

Trachtenberg, Joshua (1987). *Jewish Magic and Superstition*. Atheneum. New York.

Treadgold, Warren (1997) *A History of the Byzantine State and Society*. Stanford. US

Turner, Alice, K. (1993) *The History of Hell*. Robert Hale. London.

Walter, Philippe (2007) *Christianity; The origins of a Pagan Religion*. Inner Traditions. Vermont

Walker, D.P. (2000) *Spiritual and Demonic Magic*. Penn. US

Weyer, Johann (1577/1991). *Witches, Devils and Doctors in the Renaissance*. Center for Medieval and Early Renaissance Studies. University of New York. NY

Wilby, Emma (2005) *Cunning Folk and Familiar Spirits*. Sussex Academic Press. UK

Notes

1. See here in particular René Guénon's 'Traditional Forms & Cosmic Cycles' (1970/ 2001), 'The Lord of the World' (1927/1983), G.G. Stroumsa; 'Another Seed' (1997) and my own 'Invisible Fire' (2010)

2. See Peter Guralnick's 'The Life and legend of the " King of the Delta Blues Singers". (1998)

3. Frisvold: 'Arts of the Night' (2009) and Ankarloo & Henningsen (ed.): Early Modern European Witchcraft (1990)

4. See here Henry Maguire: 'Byzantine Magic' that discusses the role of the evil eye and also the relationship between the demonic and Judaism in the 5th Century A.D.

5. It was common to refer to the 'black books, as 'Cyprians' in Scandinavia, and in particular in Norway between the 15th and 18th Century, see for instance 'Svarteboka' edited by T. Å. Bringsværd in 1976 .

6. In A. Chr. Bang: 'Norske Hexeformularer'. (1902)

7. Ibid.

8. See for instance J. Sharpe: 'Instruments of Darkness'

9. See Ankarloo & Clark's 'Witchcraft and magic in Europe. The Middle Ages' (2002)

10. See Cavendish: 'The Powers of Evil' (1975)

11. Celestial hierarchies, p. 7

12. Celestial hierarchies p. 21

13. Churrton 2007: 47

14. See Emma Wilby; Cunning folk and familiar spirits (2005)

15. Ficions Hymns of Orpheus opens the hymn to the Moon in the following way:

Lunae Thymiama Aromata, Audi dea regina, **lucifera**, diva Luna, Tauricornis Mene, noctu currens, aerivaga,Nocturna, facitenens, puella, bene stellata, Luna, [translate]

16. In Ante-Nicene Fathers, Vol. 6. Edited by Alexander Roberts, James Donaldson, and A. Cleveland Coxe. (1886)

17. See Wilby (2005) p. 86

18. Kittredge's 'Witchcraft in Old and New England' (1929) p. 275

19. Ginzburg's Ecstasies: Deciphering the Witches' Sabbath (1991) p. 154

20. Witchcraft in Old and New England' (1929

21. Ibid. 244

22. Keith Thomas' Religion and the Decline of Magic' (1971) p. 599

23. Ibid. 612

24. Private correspondence

25. In Tillyard's 'The Elizabethean World Picture' (1942)

26. In Robert Taylor's (trans.) 'Iamblichus' Life of Pythagoras' (1986)

27. Published in the collection of texts by Bruno called 'Cause, Principle and Unity' (1998)

28. ibid

29. See Thomas Taylor's 'The Hymns of Orpheus' (1981) p 115

30. In Joseph Dan's (ed.) 'The Early Kabbalah'

31. Book One, Chapter 24

32. Sacred sexual communion, one of the five sacraments in the tantric panchamakara ritual.

33. In Maguire (ed) 'Byzantine Magic' (2008) p. 79

Index

A

Abel *11, 48, 131*
Adam *11, 54*
Alexander *13, 36, 37, 178*
Ancestors *47, 56, 59, 68, 115, 132, 139*
Angels *12, 13, 26, 27, 28, 53, 54, 102, 103, 105, 131, 134, 137*
Anwynn *57, 60*
Axis mundi *34, 38, 120*

B

Benandanti *64, 81*
Bible *64*

C

Cain *8, 10, 11, 33, 34, 48, 50, 51, 55, 63, 134, 137*
Christ *50, 51, 83*
Church *18, 19, 26, 27, 40, 41, 58, 59, 78, 83, 84, 87, 170*
Circe *162, 163, 164, 165*
Cochrane, Robert *60*
Commonwealth, The Secret *60*
Compass *8, 132*
Cross *15, 17, 20, 40, 41, 42, 45, 50,* *68, 69, 70, 72, 95, 113, 131, 134*
Crossroad *11, 15, 16, 17, 19, 20, 21, 24, 25, 30, 32, 33, 34, 39, 42, 43, 45, 55, 76, 83, 117, 134, 169, 170*
Culsans *39, 40*
Curses *85, 88, 108*

D

Daimon *10, 126*
Death *16, 20, 25, 36, 71*
Demeter *38, 149*
Demons *19, 26, 27, 67, 83, 84, 105, 107, 140, 145*
Destiny *129, 174*
Devil *9, 15, 16, 17, 18, 20, 25, 26, 27, 28, 29, 30, 32, 33, 34, 42, 43, 44, 45, 59, 61, 77, 79, 83, 92, 138, 139, 140, 169, 170*
Diana *39, 52, 67, 83*
Dionysus *8, 12, 38, 51, 52, 75*
Divination *30, 34, 67, 84, 85, 129*
Djinn *65, 66*
Dragon *45, 49, 156, 157*

E

Elphame *12, 58, 59, 66, 67, 96*
Enoch, The Book of *51*
Eros *5, 13, 98, 100, 101, 102, 107, 108, 115, 117, 147, 154, 164*
Esu *16, 25, 32*
Eve *11*
Exu *21, 33*

F

Faery *12*
Fairy *60, 61, 62, 65, 71, 93, 172*
Familiars *56, 63, 64, 79, 82, 90*
Fascinatio *18, 114*
Faunus *30, 31, 32, 40, 96*
Fortuna *39, 103*
Freya *34, 76, 91, 95, 146, 147, 165*

G

God *18, 25, 26, 27, 34, 36, 48, 51, 52, 60, 68, 74, 75, 87, 88, 98, 101, 102, 104, 106, 107, 121, 123, 125, 151, 169, 170*
Goddess *153, 154, 155, 175*
Grigori *82*

H

Hecate *24, 39, 149, 164*
Hel *60, 67, 76, 91,*

94, 96, 146, 150
Heresy 18, 78
Hermes 32, 33, 39,
   40, 62, 123,
   149, 163, 173
Holda 67, 76, 90, 95,
   96

I

Incubi 62
Ishtar 76, 146, 154,
   163, 165

J

Janus 24, 35, 39, 40,
   42
Jupiter 38, 67, 103

L

Lamia 85
Lares 31
Lilith 24, 47, 52, 55,
   85, 117, 144,
   145, 163, 165
Love 32, 41, 62, 67,
   75, 76, 84, 98,
   100, 106, 107,
   108, 110, 139,
   147, 152, 154,
   155, 159, 162,
   163, 164, 165,
   166
Lucifer 12, 13, 25,
   26, 30, 50, 52,
   75, 163
Lumiel 12, 50, 51
Lycaeus 148

M

Malefica 16, 27, 79,
   113, 115, 116,
   151
Mars 38, 113, 115,

123, 125
Medea 162, 163, 164,
   165
Mercury 33, 34, 38,
   39, 94
Moon 23, 39, 68, 75,
   76, 77, 94, 95,
   96, 120, 123,
   135, 144, 145,
   148, 150, 151,
   152, 153, 156,
   157, 159, 165,
   169, 174, 177

N

Necromancy 39, 64,
   67, 72, 149
Nephilim 58
Nocturnal 7, 82

O

Occulta Philosophia 89,
   104, 110, 150
Odin 32, 33, 34, 56,
   91, 147, 150
Orion 91
Orpheus 62, 144, 149,
   177, 178

P

Pacts 25, 82, 83, 85
Pan 30, 31, 32, 40,
   51
Picatrix 122, 123, 151
Plato 11, 100, 102,
   119, 126
Plotinus 32, 61, 102
Proserpina 62

Q

Qayin 47, 52

S

Sabbath 12, 15, 21,
   64, 67, 77, 78,
   79, 80, 84, 86,
   93, 94, 146,
   173, 178
Satan 12, 13, 17, 18,
   26, 27, 29, 30,
   41, 60, 75, 82,
   83, 85, 173
Saturn 36, 38, 115,
   123, 124, 133,
   146, 148
Seth 8, 11, 48, 50,
   54, 131
Sex 20, 51, 143
Solomon 23, 24, 90,
   173
Spells 21, 85, 108,
   109, 110
St Peter 112
Stregoni 91
Succubi 62
Sun 38, 39, 52, 74,
   75, 76, 95, 130,
   131, 144, 153,
   154, 155, 156,
   162, 163, 165,
   169

T

Talismans 109, 122

V

Vampire 18, 91, 144,
   146, 147, 150,
   151, 155
Venus 5, 12, 13, 34,
   38, 62, 74, 75,
   76, 77, 90, 91,
   93, 94, 95, 96,
   98, 108, 110,
   134, 135, 144,

145, 146, 151,
154, 156, 162,
163, 165, 166,
167, 169
Vodou 19, 20, 107,
111

W

Watchers 13
Winds 131, 137
Witchblood 159
Witches 15, 18, 21,
48, 58, 64, 67,
68, 77, 78, 80,
84, 85, 86, 92,
111, 137, 165,
173, 175, 176,
178

Z

Zeus 13, 37, 85, 148,
149, 164